TWAYNE'S WORLD AUTHORS SERIES

A Survey of the World's Literature

POLAND

Irene Nagurski

EDITOR

Witold Gombrowicz

TWAS 510

Witold Gombrowicz

WITOLD GOMBROWICZ

By EWA M. THOMPSON

Rice University

TWAYNE PUBLISHERS
A DIVISION OF G. K. HALL & CO., BOSTON

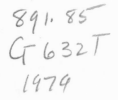
Copyright © 1979 by G. K. Hall & Co.

Published in 1979 by Twayne Publishers,
A Division of G. K. Hall & Co.

Printed on permanent/durable acid-free paper and bound
in the United States of America

First Printing

Library of Congress Cataloging in Publication Data

Thompson, Ewa Majewska.
Witold Gombrowicz.

(Twayne's world author series ; TWAS 510 : Poland)
Bibliography: pp. 163–68
Includes index.
1. Gombrowicz, Witold—Criticism and interpretation.
PG7158.G6692T48   891.8'5'37   78–15571
ISBN 0–8057–6351–1

To Congresswoman Barbara Jordan

Contents

About the Author

Ewa M. Thompson took her degrees in Poland (University of Warsaw) and the United States (Vanderbilt University). She is the author of *Russian Formalism and Anglo-American New Criticism: A Comparative Study* (1971) and of many articles on modern literature. She has taught at Indiana University, University of Virginia, University of Warsaw and Rice University. Presently, she is Professor of Russian Literature at Rice University.

Preface

Witold Gombrowicz, Polish novelist and playwright, spent most of his creative life in Argentina where he was stranded in 1939 when World War II broke out in Europe. When he left Poland in 1939 he was considered a promising young man; when he left Argentina to return to Europe, he was a widely acclaimed avant-garde writer whose eccentricity and narrative talent won him both friends and enemies. Today, Gombrowicz is regarded as the most significant Polish writer to emerge after World War II. His influence on Polish prose and theatre has been enormous and his popularity in Europe and the United States continues to grow. In 1967, he was awarded the International Publishers' Prize.

This book has been written as a concise analysis of Gombrowicz's literary works. Chapter One provides information about Gombrowicz's life. Chapters Two, Three, Four, and Five discuss his short stories, plays, novels and the *Journal*; the following four chapters deal with those facets of Gombrowicz's works which are characteristic of all his writings and require separate treatment. Chapter Ten presents what appears to be Gombrowicz's literary universe: the world in which his characters live.

I have used the following principles in matters of quotation, translation and footnoting: all the material quoted is footnoted except quotations from the Polish *Collected Works* (*Dzieła Zebrane*). This last edition is identified by volume number and page after quotation. The translations are mine. Second, unless, for some specific reason, it was necessary to do otherwise, I have used the anglicized names of characters as they appear in the existing English translations. Where there was no translation, I have used the most likely rendition from Polish to English. Thus *Trans-Atlantyk* becomes *Trans-Atlantic*, and *Gonzalo* becomes *Gonzalez*. Third, I have quoted from existing

WITOLD GOMBROWICZ

translations unless they are inadequate for my purposes or do not exist. In such cases, I have translated directly from the Polish text and indicated this in parentheses by giving the volume number and page from *Dzieła Zebrane* (*Collected Works*). In the few cases where it was absolutely necessary to quote the Polish text, I did so.

I would like to express my gratitude to those persons who in many ways contributed to the preparation of this book: the editor of *Kultura*, Jerzy Giedroyć; Professor Czesław Miłosz of the University of California at Berkeley; Professor Michał Głowiński of the Polish Academy of Sciences in Warsaw; the editor of *The Polish Review*, Ludwik Krzyżanowski; and Rita Gombrowicz. My thanks also are due to Rice University for a research grant which enabled me to make a trip to Poland and France in search of Gombrowicziana and to my editors at G. K. Hall: Irene Nagurski and Jerry Kantor, for valuable suggestions and careful editing. Finally, I would like to acknowledge permission to quote from the works of Gombrowicz published by Institut Littéraire, Grove Press and Temple University Press.

EWA M. THOMPSON

Houston and Princeton

Chronology

1904   Witold Marian Gombrowicz born August 4 on his parents' estate at Małoszyce in southeast Poland.

1915   Family moves to Warsaw.

1916–   Attends Wielopolski Gymnasium, an exclusive secondary
1922   school in Warsaw.

1923–   Reads law at the University of Warsaw.
1926

1926–   Travels in France. Attends *l'Institut des Hautes Etudes*
1927   *Internationales* in Paris.

1928   Begins his apprenticeship in the municipal court in Warsaw. Writes "Kraykowski's Dancer," "The Memoir of Stefan Czarniecki," "Premeditated Murder," "Virginity."

1929–   Writes "Symposium at Countess Kotłubaj's," "Adven-
1932   tures," "The Kitchen Stairs," "Events on H.M.S. Banbury."

1933   Publication of *Memoir from Adolescence* containing the short stories written in 1928–1932.

1934–   Abandons law for a writing career.
1939

1935   *Ivona, Princess of Burgundia*

1937   *Ferdydurke.*

1939   Trip to Argentina. Lands in Buenos Aires on August 22.

1939–   Penniless existence in Buenos Aires. In order to survive,
1947   borrows money and does hack work for local newspapers.

1947–   Works as secretary at the Banco Polaco in Buenos Aires.
1955

1947   *The Marriage* published in Spanish in Buenos Aires.

1953   *Trans-Atlantic* and *The Marriage* published in Polish by Institut Littéraire (Paris) which had since become Gombrowicz's major publisher. The *Journal* begins to appear in installments in the monthly *Kultura.*

1955   Quits his job at the bank and devotes himself to writing full time.

1957– *Ferdydurke, Trans-Atlantic, The Marriage* and the short
1958   stories (*Bakakaj*) republished in Poland.
1957   *Journal 1953–1956.*
1960   *Pornografia.*
1961   Receives the *Kultura* Literary Award.
1962   *Journal 1957–1961.*
1963   Awarded the Ford Fellowship for Writers. Returns to
       Europe.
1965   *Cosmos.*
1966   *Journal 1961–1966. Operetta.*
1967   Awarded International Publishers' Prize for *Cosmos.*
1969   Dies July 24 in Vence, France, of respiratory troubles
       and heart failure.

CHAPTER 1

In Place of a Biography

IN 1904 Witold Gombrowicz was born into a family of Polish squierarchy. His father ran the family estate at Małoszyce and occupied managerial positions in various industries. When Gombrowicz was eight years old, his parents sold the estate and moved to Warsaw. There the family settled into an upper middle class pattern of living. Its members were well educated and took interest in literature, the arts and other forms of cultural life which the city provided. All this was done in moderation. By virtue of their background and occupation, the Gombrowiczes were consumers rather than creators of culture. They stood apart from the people genuinely dedicated to thought and from the Polish artistic *avant-garde* which was, like its counterpart in western Europe at that time, engaged in the search for radically new ways of artistic expression. The Gombrowiczes sent their children to the best schools, hired teachers to teach them languages and music, attended cultural events with them—and hoped that literature and the arts would remain pastimes rather than become the professions of their children. Their hopes were fulfilled to a large extent, since three of their four children followed in their footsteps and accepted their values and way of life. Only Witold took a different course.

Gombrowicz's family was by no means as stable and socially secure as might at first appear. Within the Polish context it was a family which did not fit comfortably in any of the three major social groups: the landed nobility who were a notch above them; the peasantry and poor city dwellers whose social status was infinitely lower; or the monied bourgeoisie lacking refinement and distinguished ancestry, but whose sources of income were closest to those of the Gombrowiczes. This family shared the petty vanities and social insecurities of the French

13

plutocracy which Proust describes in *Remembrance of Things Past:* they aspired to being aristocrats while they were, in fact, members of the upper middle class. They wanted to preserve the vestiges of another epoch, while owing their comfortable existence to the opportunities provided by the new times.

In one of his autobiographical sketches Gombrowicz ascribed only to himself the discomfort of knowing the life of his family was a make-believe life, that it was "a school of unreality." This was probably an exaggeration; he tended to underrate the sensitivity and perceptions of those who surrounded him in his early years. It would be more accurate to say that he inherited a sense of the uncertainty of his origins and magnified this uncertainty in his own mind to such an extent that it became a distinguishing feature of his art and personality.

As a beginning writer, he felt alien to the milieu of Polish squierarchy who still avidly read Henryk Sienkiewicz and other nineteenth-century realists, native and foreign. He regarded them as simple-minded and hopelessly removed from the problems of the day, and liked to tease them by expressing outrageous—to their way of thinking—opinions. He sought shelter from them among his artistic friends from the literary cafés in Warsaw with whom he spent many an evening drinking coffee and discussing literature and contemporary thought. In his essay on Sienkiewicz written many years later, he dismissed members of the gentry as "an irredeemable herd of idle oafs" (VI, 299). However, the artists with whom he associated in Warsaw were a mixed lot; some of them came from proletarian backgrounds which he, the product of a genteel milieu, found hardly to his taste. Before them he boasted of his noble ancestors. In the autobiographical note which he prepared for *L'Herne* in 1969, he flaunted his noble origins with the assumed naiveté of a *nouveau riche* displaying his recently acquired sophistication.[1]

We learn from it that as a child he was taught French by a governess; that he traveled yearly to Germany and Austria with his mother; that his school was packed with the children of aristocrats; that his butler rather than he attended the lectures at the law school whenever Gombrowicz did not feel like leaving the house. In the *Journal* (*Dziennik*) he confessed to a feeling of awkwardness when meeting people of truly princely origins. In *A Kind of Testament* he observed that his family was an uprooted one and that its social position was not quite clear: it stood "between land and industry, between what is known as 'good society' and another, more middle-class society."[2] From the time when as a boy he started to play with peasant children he began to hate the drawing room and secretly adore the kitchen, the pantry, the stable and those who belonged there. "Degradation became my ideal forever.... But I did not realize that by worshipping the slave I became an aristocrat."[3]

These identity vacillations of early youth were never abandoned. Many years after the events described above, an acquaintance of Gombrowicz from Buenos Aires remarked that in Argentina Gombrowicz behaved in a similar way. When in the company of writers and intellectuals he stressed his connections with the landed gentry, whereas in the company of aristocrats he expressed contempt for the privileges of birth.[4] These self-conscious statements whose sentiments range from petty vanity and resentment to defiant sincerity are very characteristic of Gombrowicz's values and shortcomings as a writer. He sees human beings as warriors who try to impose their vision of the world on others. His pitiless lucidity perceives the pose where others still see sincerity. His understanding of resentment and rancor is profound. What is even rarer, he does not put this understanding at the service of a moralistic purpose. He accepts this resentful humanity and takes great pains in the *Journal* to show himself a part of it. He plays the role of devil's advocate at his own expense.

In 1926, Gombrowicz went to France for one and a half years. He attended l'Institut des Hautes Études Internationales in Paris and traveled around the country. He was completely alone. No friends or family accompanied him, and he was not enough distinguished either by birth or achievement to be noticed. He speaks sparingly of his experiences as a lone traveler. Occasionally, he remarks that he kept bad company. It appears that this solitary trip intensified his feeling of alienation. The boy who in school felt that he did not belong was likely to experience even stronger feelings of estrangement in an unfamiliar milieu.

The outsider syndrome was nurtured in Gombrowicz not only by the uncertainty of his origins and position in the world but also, and primarily, by his psychological predisposition. His school friend Tadeusz Kępiński said about him that already at an early age he suffered from an atrophy of tenderness. Gombrowicz once remarked in the *Journal* that he did not know how to love. His acquaintances and he himself agree that Gombrowicz was never emotionally open with his parents and siblings, and that he maintained a distance between himself and his friends. Kępiński also recalls that as a teenager, Gombrowicz used to laugh at the idea of marrying and having children. It might have been a reaction to the conflict which existed between his parents and which he took very much to heart as a child. Characteristically, there are no deep love relationships in his books. He married at age sixty-four, shortly before his death. In *A Kind of Testament* he said that he felt in himself a secret flaw and that he was always "outside the human herd."[5] He never trusted anyone enough to dissolve this secret in friendship. In his book on Gombrowicz, Kępiński tries hard to present him in a sympathetic light: in spite of his efforts, his remembrances add up to the picture of a sickly, secretive and self-centered person who often tried the patience of those around him.[6]

Writing, at first, was also a secret affair. Gombrowicz began to write in high school, but did not show his first attempts to anyone. (He maintained the habit of destroying first drafts until he died.) Yet Gombrowicz worked furiously at style. He said later that beginning at age sixteen, he read philosophy and literature mainly to acquire mastery over words and to become "like the great writers." Only in his mid-twenties, when he began working on the short stories which later appeared in *Memoir from Adolescence* (*Pamiętnik z okresu dojrzewania*, 1933), did his secretiveness give way to common sense, and he sought advice from newly acquired literary acquaintances, as well as his school friends Tadeusz Kępiński and Stanisław Baliński.[7] The latter was a member of the poetic group *Skamander* which played an important role in Polish literary life between the two world wars. He was an authority for Gombrowicz, a few years older, already recognized for his literary talent and conversational brilliance. Baliński offered plenty of advice and eventually wrote on the published copy of the *Memoir* which belonged to Kępiński: ". . . this book profited enormously from my instruction and corrections; I helped to arrange its publication; in short, the book owes its existence to my help."[8] It is easy to imagine Gombrowicz's reaction to this jocular display of self-assurance. The feeling of envy and resentment toward his older and ultimately less illustrious colleague never left him. Outwardly, they remained friends and corresponded until Gombrowicz died.

Memoir from Adolescence was published the way many first books are published: friends and family pitched in and provided material and moral support. Baliński not only read and corrected the manuscript but also invented the title. Gombrowicz's father came up with half the money for publishing costs. The book came out in the well known publishing house Rój in Warsaw which specialized in fiction and put out many successful novels between the two world wars. When the book appeared, Gombrowicz was anxious to find out what his closest acquaintances thought about it. He and Kępiński discussed the *Memoir* in letters, and they exchanged copies of the book with remarks written on the margins. These exchanges show Gombrowicz as both eager and cautious, spontaneous and self-conscious in matters concerning his literary career.

Gombrowicz's first book received mixed reviews. Praised by Leon Piwiński, a critic, and Jerzy Andrzejewski, a fellow writer, it was criticized by others for its alleged immaturity. This last group of critics invoked the word *dojrzewanie* (immaturity, adolescence) which appeared in the title. Gombrowicz soon realized that the title solicited unkind remarks: if the author insists on calling himself immature, it is unlikely that the critics will resist the temptation of agreeing. Gombrowicz's reaction to criticism was anything but conciliatory. He complained that he had been criticized by "cultural aunties" who could chit-chat about literature but were unable to understand serious writers like himself.[9] Apparently he decided to spite his critics and devote his next book to the celebration of immaturity. He seemed to say, "Immature? Well, I shall show them that greenness can be a valid point of view in the novel." Thus, later in *A Kind of Testament* Gombrowicz maintains that out of such attitudes *Ferdydurke* was born.

Everything considered, Gombrowicz's artistic debut was successful. The book was noticed and it assured him a place in the literary cafés and in the minds of people interested in new talents. It also launched him on his journalistic career. Between 1933 and 1939 Gombrowicz wrote a great number of feuilletons and reviews for such periodicals as *Kurier Poranny* (*The Morning News*), *Gazeta Polska* (*The Polish Gazette*), *Polska Zbrojna* (*Poland in Arms*), *Czas* (*Time*), *Prosto z Mostu* (*The Plain Dealer*) and *Wiadomości Literackie* (*The Literary Review*). With the exception of *Wiadomości*, all these journals were mildly or strongly conservative. *Wiadomości*, by no means an avant-garde journal, represented the middle-of-the-road tendency in regard to literary innovation. Gombrowicz, who occasionally liked to pretend he was a radical both in social and literary views, did not find it disturbing to publish in these periodicals. Why? Partly, it was a matter of opportunity. Upon the publication of the *Memoir* he received an offer to write four articles a year for *Polska Zbrojna* and accepted it. The story was similar with other journals. More important, his choices of places in which to publish were accidental. He was a loner, a private and secretive person who stepped aside from trends, tendencies and programs. It was all the same to him where he published. Gombrowicz liked to think of himself as a person outside the constraints of ideology and thus free to print books anywhere. His first play *Ivona, Princess of Burgundia* (*Iwona, Księżniczka Burgunda*, 1935) appeared in *Skamander*, yet he never joined the Skamandrites. In fact, he never belonged to any literary group in Poland or abroad.

An incident he relates in his reminiscences lends still another dimension to his dislike of being a joiner. During years of frequenting literary cafés, he often had an opportunity to sit at the table usually occupied by well known Skamandrites. He never availed himself of this opportunity. Instead, he established a table of his own and invited other beginning writers to sit with him. Gombrowicz's excessive aversion to membership in any group, however, went hand in hand with a desire to be the center of a group. His persistence and dedication could have produced another literary "ism" had the potential leader and members not been "deactivated" by the war. In the meantime, Gombrowicz's solitary ways had adverse consequences too. He had relatively few literary friends or well-wishers interested in providing him with constructive criticism or in facilitating the business of publishing.

Tadeusz Kępiński was one of those who inspired Gombrowicz's confidence thanks to his jovial, unassuming manner and lack of writing ambitions. Gombrowicz's and Kępiński's parents were friends and the two boys had met at an early age. As adults they corresponded for years. In the 1930s they decided to write a detective story together, "a novel for scullery maids," as Gombrowicz liked to emphasize. He saw the venture as a stylistic exercise, part of his investigation into the secret of success of the Polish romance writer Helena Mniszek whose novel *The Leper (Trędowata)* was, in his opinion, so perfectly bad that it deserved to be called a classic among bad novels. The collaboration did not last long. Eventually, Gombrowicz wrote *The Possessed (Opętani)* all by himself. In 1939 it began to appear in installments in two daily newspapers, and was signed Zdzisław Niewieski to distinguish it from Gombrowicz's serious works.

The Possessed is a romance, a horror story and a detective story all in one. Relying heavily on the supernatural and using the boy-meets-girl plot, it is a compendium of the most worn out clichés in the Polish language. The plot is easy to follow and presented according to the principles of nineteenth-century realism: the impersonal and omniscient narrator tells the story of one group of characters but then forsakes the group to narrate another story about another group of characters.

The theme and technique of *The Possessed* are very different from the rest of Gombrowicz's works. At first, the novel seems to be a long and elaborate joke, something in the vein of Magdalena Samozwaniec's *On the Lips of Sin (Na ustach grzechu*, 1922). However, given Gombrowicz's interest in "the refuse rooms" of human minds, it is also a deliberate encounter with the second-rate and an attempt to find out why it fascinates so many people. A recent critic discovered in *The Possessed* the germ of *Pornografia* (1960).[10] In his view, both books are parodies of the country novel popular in Poland for many decades. Both plots revolve around two youngsters of different sexes who finally begin to like each other owing to the machinations of a "pornographer" and their own wayward instincts. Doubtless writing *The Possessed* taught Gombrowicz how to construct pleasant-sounding phrases and entertain. He used this self-taught lesson in his later works where instead of hackneyed expressions we find new rhythms of speech. He preserved, however, the tendency to entertain, only replacing sentimental romance with burlesque humor.

In 1934 Gombrowicz resigned from his job at the municipal court and devoted himself entirely to writing. As a side occupation he took up the management of an apartment building which belonged to his family. This gave him the means of livelihood. In 1938 he had good reason to look confidently to the future. He was author of *Princess Ivona* and *Ferdydurke*, was considered an interesting literary figure, and was full of energy and the desire to keep writing. Soon afterwards, all these advantages became meaningless. In 1939, his literary career came to a crashing halt.

A few weeks before World War II broke out, Gombrowicz boarded the Polish ship "Chrobry" sailing to Argentina on its first cruise. For publicity reasons two young writers had been invited to travel free of charge. One of them was Gombrowicz. News of the war came just as the ship landed in Buenos Aires. The passengers found themselves abandoned in a foreign land, their positions, money, and all paraphernalia of living gone. They faced the choice of returning to Europe (the ship eventually sailed to England) and joining the Polish Army-in-exile, or staying in Argentina and letting the chips fall where they might. They could not return to Poland which after a month of bloody fighting was overrun by German troops.

In the time-honored Polish tradition of patriotic zeal, Gombrowicz went to the Polish embassy in Buenos Aires and underwent a medical examination to determine his fitness for military service. Classified 4-F, he then decided not to return to Europe but to start a new life in Argentina. It was an adventuresome decision. He had never known the lower depths of existence; yet now he was faced with the necessity of struggling for survival. His previous literary career counted for naught in a country whose language he hardly knew and where his books had never been published. To continue writing was out of the question. What to do? He had about two hundred dollars to his name. He lived on this money for half a year. Then, as he put it in an autobiographical sketch, he began to get by on his wits. Gombrowicz borrowed money, tried to write features for Argentinian newspapers, and received some money from the Polish embassy. Then he tried to borrow again. Those who write about this period in Gombrowicz's life usually refrain from exposing the details of his humiliating and penniless existence. He was spared few indignities during those years.[11]

Gombrowicz's acquaintances in Argentina, Jeremi Stępowski in particular, introduced him to the important figures in Argentinian cultural life: Manuel Galvez, Arturo Capdevila, Roger Pla, Antonio Berni, Victoria Ocampo, Ernesto Sabato and Carlos Mastronardi. The poet Mastronardi was the only person with whom Gombrowicz struck any kind of friendship. He offended or shocked others by his refusal to play a role in the social game, a game well defined by the circumstances of life: these people were powerful and he was powerless; he was recognized in Poland, perhaps, but not in the capitals of the western world. Gombrowicz did not observe the rules of the pecking order.

Gombrowicz's *Journal* contains descriptions of how he disappointed the Capdevilas at a dinner in their house when he refused to mouth the clichés expected of a civilized European, and how he insulted Enrique Larreta by comparing Larreta's antique furniture bought in an art shop to similar antiques inherited by his, Gombrowicz's, family, from a long line of ancestors.[12] The Argentinian *Journal* also abounds in sarcastic remarks about the art patroness Victoria Ocampo. In short, in Argentina as well as in Poland, Gombrowicz was the opposite of a social charmer. He displayed his rough edges even in the presence of people whose good will he desperately needed.

These experiences strengthened his conviction that the "essence" of a person is a contentless concept. Human beings are formed by their contacts with other human beings and by the pressures and privileges which these contacts create. This interaction is the only reality—there is no other. Gombrowicz's fic-

tional world reflects this belief. What matters in it is the interaction of individuals rather than the individuals themselves.
Characters try to mold one another into the creatures of their
wishes. What counts is who will subjugate whom to his or her
desires, whims and opinions. Gombrowicz's world is not "nice":
it arises out of grim struggle. Like his countryman Jerzy Kosiński,
Gombrowicz writes primarily about the load of hostility which
nice persons carry within themselves and which they unload
on other nice persons. In his fiction and in critical pronouncements Gombrowicz championed his artistic vision with fervor
and obstinacy. He first conceived it in Poland; his Argentinian
circumstances, accidental though they at first seemed, turned
out to be an ideal testing ground.

Gombrowicz's relations with the cultural establishment in
Buenos Aires broke off after he refused to play the role of
poor relative. He fared better in proletarian circles which he
first entered of necessity and later, by choice. In the Morón
district of Buenos Aires where he played many a game of check-
ers and where he earned many a meal in so doing, he met the
"other" Argentina: young, unrefined and unadulterated (as he
put it) by a minimal admixture of European culture. We know
very little of this side of Gombrowicz's life. What he tells us
in the Journal is, obviously, well sifted out, and his acquaintances
from Morón were not the kind who write memoirs. They remain a voiceless presence in Gombrowicz's life. Yet Gombrowicz maintains that the familiarity he enjoyed among his
unrefined Argentinian friends had a profound influence on his
artistic development. It solidified his other belief: that relationships between people are governed also by a secret desire
for, and envy of, youth, immaturity, crudity and primitiveness.
This belief is evident in Ferdydurke in Pimko's sexual longings
and the readiness of the Youthfuls to worship those younger
than they. It becomes central in Pornografia (1960) and in
Operetta (1966).

Gombrowicz's first seven years in Argentina were lean ones,
in many ways a reversal of his previous mode of existence.
In the district of Buenos Aires where he lived, there were no
literary cafés where financially secure young artists could
discuss their books and paintings. It was difficult to think of

publishing while living in small hotels and not knowing where the next meal was coming from. When the war was over, Gombrowicz's troubles did not end. In spite of his lack of interest in politics, he could not bring himself to go back to Poland and accept its new political status. Yet he realized that if he stayed in Argentina, he would have to start all over again and go through all the uncertainties and agonies to which a beginning writer is exposed.

Gombrowicz chose to accept the difficulties and risks entailed in remaining in Argentina. At the age of forty he wrote his second play *The Marriage* (*Ślub*) and the short story "The Banquet" ("Bankiet"). *The Marriage* was published in Spanish in 1947 with the Argentinian art patroness Cecilia Debenedetti sponsoring the translation. In 1964, again through the financial help of Debenedetti, *Ferdydurke* appeared in Spanish. By then, however, it had already appeared in western Europe and the United States.

1947 was a lucky year for Gombrowicz. Not only did he publish the new play, his first major work in years, but he was also offered a job at the newly established Banco Polaco in Buenos Aires. He later said that his main occupation at the bank was writing *Trans-Atlantic*. His co-workers confirm this. One of them recalls that years later, he tried to find at least one document—a memo, a note, a report—signed by Gombrowicz, but could not find any.[13] It appears that a tacit agreement existed between Gombrowicz and his employers: the job was to be a sinecure allowing him time to work on literary projects.

At that time Gombrowicz began to correspond with the editor of *Kultura,* the Polish language literary journal published in Paris. In 1948, he began to publish in *Kultura.* The novel *Trans-Atlantic* published there was his third "debut" and eventually led to the recognition of Gombrowicz as a significant European writer. At the time when *Trans-Atlantic* was first published, however, Gombrowicz acquired notoriety rather than success. His apparent lack of respect for the tragic realities of the recent war evoked violently negative reactions. Many people felt insulted by *Trans-Atlantic* and vented their outrage in letters to *Kultura* and articles published elsewhere. To appease the indignant readers, Józef Wittlin, a highly respected writer, wrote a preface to the book edition of *Trans-Atlantic*. He argued there that Gombrowicz wanted to demolish the mystifications of history rather than sneer at virtue, and that the book was an eye opener and an energy raiser. Wittlin's positive opinion eventually prevailed: in two decades, *Trans-Atlantic* was to become a classic of Polish literature.

In 1955, Gombrowicz quit his job at Banco Polaco, and once more devoted himself entirely to writing. The period 1953-1966 was the most productive in his life. During this time he published two novels, one play, and three volumes of the *Journal*. These thirteen years can be compared to the preceding thirteen which brought one novel, one play and several short stories. The "thaw" in eastern Europe was beneficial to him also, since it made it possible for him to publish in Poland. Within a year— 1956-1957—all his works with the exception of the *Journal* appeared in Poland where they met with huge success. Until then, he had been a legendary figure there: his pre-war *Ferdydurke* was a bibliographical rarity and his post-war writings were available only to the lucky few, as *emigré* publications cannot be freely distributed in Poland.

One critic recalls that he once missed a long distance train because he saw a copy of *Ferdydurke* in the window of a second hand bookstore, and he stopped to buy it. Now, for a few weeks at least (all Polish editions of Gombrowicz were out of print within that period of time, and second printings never came), anybody could buy his works. *Princess Ivona* was performed in Cracow in 1957 and later in other Polish cities. All of a sudden, Gombrowicz became a major writer. His irreverent tone, the rough but precise rhythm of his prose, and the novelty of his topics became fashionable and popular. In other countries his reception went much the same way, although on a smaller scale. His plays were performed in Paris (*The Marriage*, 1964, *Princess Ivona*, 1965), in Berlin (*The Marriage*, 1968) and in Stockholm (*Princess Ivona*, 1965). His novels were translated into all major European languages. Success came to Gombrowicz also in the form of literary prizes and awards. First came the *Kultura* Literary Prize (1961), then the London *Wiadomości* Prize for the *Journal* (1963) and the

Ford Foundation Grant for Writers (1963). In 1967 he was awarded the International Publishers' Prize.

In the 1950s, a small but dedicated group of admirers and supporters began to gather around him. Among them were the *Kultura* editor Jerzy Giedroyć, the French critic of Polish descent Constantin Jeleński and the young Frenchman Dominique de Roux whose friendship inspired an important book on Gombrowicz: *A Kind of Testament* (written by Gombrowicz himself and first published in *Kultura* as fragments of the *Journal*[14]). Gombrowicz often emphasized that were it not for Jeleński, he would have remained an obscure *emigré* writer. The same could be said about Giedroyć who believed in Gombrowicz's talent long before the latter became famous. At present, a reasonably complete collection of Gombrowicz's works is available in major European languages. *Trans-Atlantic* and the *Journal* are not yet available in English. The former is extraordinarily difficult to translate because of its blend of archaisms and neologisms, the liberties it takes with grammar, and frequent allusions to Polish literature and customs. I cannot explain why the latter has not yet been translated into English (both are available in French and German).

In 1963, Gombrowicz left South America for the first time in twenty-four years. He spent a year in Berlin and after several months of travel settled down in the town of Vence in southern France. At the time when he became universally recognized as a writer, his health rapidly deteriorated. His visit to Berlin was interrupted by a two-months' stay in the hospital. Even earlier, he began to suffer from asthma attacks. In 1968, he had a heart attack. Several months later he died of another heart attack precipitated by respiratory troubles.

In the last months of his life he was too ill to write. Two details of this period should be mentioned to complete his biographical sketch. He married his companion of several years Rita Labrosse. The second significant event was the "course" in philosophy given by Gombrowicz to his friend Dominique de Roux. Gombrowicz who so often played the role of ignoramus in his *Journal* was now speaking with ease and without any preparation about the problems of modern philosophy and about the moral dilemmas of humanity. His account of Hegel, Schopenhauer, Husserl, Sartre and Heidegger bears no resemblance to a textbook summary. It is worth reading as an extraordinary personal response to the thoughts of philosophers whose thinking shaped this modern age.[15]

In this account of Gombrowicz's life I have purposely stressed details often glossed over in short biographies: the writer's concern with career rather than Art; his concern with the means of livelihood; the relation of success, failure, recognition or oblivion, to such seemingly arbitrary matters as the identity of one's literary agent, one's geographical location or time of birth. This approach seems consistent with Gombrowicz's personality. As Czesław Miłosz put it, Gombrowicz is an expert in "cornering the reader into an admission of unpalatable truths."[16] One of these truths is that very few writers are totally oblivious to the mundane details of life such as keeping up with the Joneses (i.e., other writers) and making a living.

Who will dare maintain that the success-failure dichotomy has not bothered those who celebrate Art with utmost devotion? It may be customary to pretend that such concerns do not exist but the very act of writing proves such pretensions false: writing is always *for someone*, even when, as René Girard says, "One writes in order to prove to the reader that one does not care about him."[17] Gombrowicz passionately believed that immunity to vanity does not exist and that literary works are firmly planted in the mundane details of artists' lives. In his *Journal* whenever he devoted some pages to theories and ideas, he always inserted a phrase like "I had a good chicken dinner today" or "The chops were excellent." In his autobiographical sketch, he wrote about his own financing of the first edition of *Ferdydurke* in French, and also quoted the amount of money he eventually made on this edition.[18] It is fitting, therefore, to portray Gombrowicz as a down-to-earth man who clumsily, stubbornly, and through many interruptions caused by external circumstances, strove to develop a unique narrative talent.

CHAPTER 2

Short Stories

I   *"Kraykowski's Dancer"*

THE hero of "Kraykowski's Dancer" ("Tancerz Mecenasa Kraykowskiego," 1928)[1] is a lonely epileptic who lives an uninteresting and shabby life. He despises, fears, and desperately needs people. His relationship with the lawyer Kraykowski—a perfectly successful man—resembles that of Dostoevsky's Man from the Underground with the nameless officer who slighted him in the street, or of the cuckolded husband to his wife's lover in Dostoevsky's "The Eternal Husband." The Dancer has been similarly offended by Kraykowski. Instead of seeking direct revenge as was the case with the Man from the Underground, he devises a complicated plan of action which is meant both to destroy Kraykowski and to satisfy his own masochistic urge. He weakens Kraykowski's composure and self-assurance by forcing him to react to his, the Dancer's, immaturity and shame. The Dancer imposes himself on Kraykowski in a variety of ways. His excitement and imbalance rub off on Kraykowski who is first annoyed, then angry, then fearful, and finally leaves the city in panic, hoping to return when the Dancer forgets about him. Needless to say, the Dancer is not about to do so.

This is a sado-masochistic story. The Dancer hurts himself no less than his victim. He is a sick and lonely man who yearns to be in contact with someone—anyone. Kraykowski takes enough interest in him to pull him by his collar away from the box office where the Dancer wanted to buy a ticket without waiting in line. Kraykowski's act is not friendly; however, it is the only display of interest the Dancer has experienced in a long time. He reacts to it in a pathological way like Pavel Pavlovich Trusotsky in "The Eternal Husband," by overwhelming his adversary with attention and submissiveness.

27

Critics often mention the similarity between Gombrowicz's Kraykowski of this story and his description of his own father in *A Kind of Testament.*[2] The similarity adds a Freudian dimension to the story. The Dancer smothers Kraykowski with attention, just as Kraykowski smothers him by possessing social qualities which the Dancer secretly aspires to have. The duel of wills brings the Dancer-Oedipus a victory: Kraykowski-Laius flees the battlefield.

II *"The Memoir of Stefan Czarniecki"*

"The Memoir of Stefan Czarniecki" ("Pamiętnik Stefana Czarnieckiego," 1928) deals with another loner whose life is spent trying to establish contact with people and failing to do so. From early youth Czarniecki craves acceptance; he wants to be accepted as a schoolmate, an aristocrat, a patriot, a soldier and a lover. Yet no one wants him. He does not belong anywhere: half-aristocrat and half-Jew, he is eager to please everyone but cannot attach himself to any community. Frustrated, he reacts violently to all traditional values, feeling that if he cannot partake of them he must destroy them. He persuades himself that family, love, patriotism and gentleness are always interlaced with phoniness. Unlike other contemporary stories which deal with frustration, "The Memoir" is not concerned with Czarniecki's anguish but with the process of trying to win others over to his way of thinking. Czarniecki's will proves to be weaker than that of his adversaries, and he fails. Again, the autobiographical element is here: tension between mother and father, between the social world of aristocracy and artistic circles, the conflict between patriotism and self-preservation—all familiar to Gombrowicz in his early years.

III *"Premeditated Murder"*

"Premeditated Murder" ("Zbrodnia z premedytacją," 1928) resembles a detective story rolling backwards. The examining magistrate visits a country home to find that the master of the house has died of a heart attack the night before. To revenge himself for the feeling of discomfort and humiliation he experi-

Banquet," he is an embarrassment to all. He shares with Princess Ivona the talent for stripping others of their pretenses. This makes him doubly embarrassing, for in addition to not being able to behave according to his station, he exposes the fact that no one in his surroundings is, in fact, worthy of his or her station either. When presented to the guests at a reception, for example, Maciek betrays his family by revealing its secrets: "And, as he followed his father (the two were very much alike, except that whatever was covered up in the father by his wits and bearing, the son displayed in great disarray, so to speak, and openly), he dragged out of him all the unpleasant details and made them public, like a dog who follows the partridges until the hunter sees them" (X, 166). Maciek unwittingly also accomplishes a similar feat in regard to his mother and brothers. So immaturity triumphs, with the debacle of the Draga family brought to completion. The center of power shifts from the assumed maturity of the Draga family to Maciek's unselfconscious immaturity.

X *"The Rat"*

"The Rat" ("Szczur," 1937) tells the story of an outlaw who combines characteristics of Robin Hood and also the Cossack rebel Stenka Razin. This archetypal outlaw murders people in broad daylight only, never stabbing anyone in the back. He despises meanness, cunning, and double dealing. Everyone likes him for his "honest" and "open" nature. He has, however, one secret enemy: the old bachelor Skorabkowski who makes it his life's task to help fulfill the letter of the law. Skorabkowski hates this criminal not so much for the murders he has committed as for his lack of inhibitions and ability freely to express wishes and thoughts. The conflict here is an example of what Gombrowicz elsewhere describes as "the miser's hatred toward the hobo." The miser wants to impose limitations on the hobo, to cut him down to size, make him into his own image. Skorabkowski devises a complicated plan to achieve this very thing. After many unsuccessful skirmishes, he finally manages to imprison the criminal in the basement of his (Skorabkowski's) house and begins to work on developing self-consciousness in

him. It turns out that the bandit is panically afraid of rats. The
taming of the bandit with the help of a rat takes up the rest
of the story.

XI   *"The Banquet"*

"The Banquet" ("Bankiet," 1944) presents another instance
of the fight of wills. The king, Gnulo, lacks royal bearing and
royal feelings. He feels and behaves like the shabbiest com-
moner. In particular, he takes petty bribes which give him more
pleasure than the big ones. The members of his council try to
instill dignity in him. Their task is to defend royalty against
Gnulo, to terrorize the greedy bribe taker with the splendor
and majesty of the Crown, to fight "for the King against the
king" (IX, 201). The fight between meanness and magnanim-
ity ends in universal chaos.

XII   *An Overview*

Memoir from Adolescence (*Pamiętnik z okresu dojrzewania*)
was first published in Poland in 1933. It was republished there
in 1957 with some changes, mostly cuts, introduced by the
author, the most substantial cut occurring in "Virginity." The
titles of some stories were also shortened: "Five Minutes Before Falling Asleep" became "Adventures," and "Events on
H.M.S. Banbury: or the State of Mind of F. Zantman" dropped
its subtitle. In addition to the seven original stories of the
Memoir, the second edition contains five more. Two of them
are fragments of *Ferdydurke*, two others appeared in *Skamander*
in 1937-1938, and one comes from the London journal *Wia-
domoś*ci (1953). The title of the second edition was changed
to *Bakakaj* to commemorate the street on which Gombrowicz
lived in Buenos Aires.

The third edition of Gombrowicz's stories came out in Paris
in 1972, as Volume 9 of his *Collected Works*. It contains all
the stories from the two previous editions with the exception
of the *Ferdydurke* fragments, and it follows the authorial cuts
of the second edition. It leaves out the stories which appeared
in the Polish press in the 1930s: they are reprinted in Volume
10 of *Collected Works* together with the feuilletons, reviews

and other occasional writings. These stories are usually very short and often seem unfinished ["The Well" ("Studnia"), "The Baron's Family Drama" ("Dramat baronostwa")]. Some are early versions of *Ferdydurke* ["Tośka," "The Mechanism of Life" ("Mechanizm życia")]. The best, "Pampelan by Radio" ("Pampelan w tubie"), is Gombrowicz's version of the Slavic folktale about the stupid Johnny who outwits his older and smarter brothers.

Gombrowicz's stories show few attempts to imitate other writers or gain writing expertise via apprenticeship. The influence of Dostoevsky visible in "Kraykowski's Dancer" and "The Memoir of Stefan Czarniecki" is tempered by a point of view quite different from one evident in *Notes from the Underground.* The stories deal with intense and determined male characters who narrate their life histories. These males are often outsiders of some kind: owing to mixed parentage (Czarniecki), epilepsy (Kraykowski's Dancer), or an extraordinary restlessness (the protagonist of "Adventures"). They are intelligent, educated, and strongly desirous of something.

In spite of this serious framework, humor is an integral part of these stories. Some of them ("Pampelan by Radio," "On the Kitchen Stairs," "The Rat," "The Banquet," "The Memoir of Stefan Czarniecki") can be read as "funny stories." Their highly formal language is so obviously at odds with the ludicrous events they describe that the incongruity evokes laughter. Here Gombrowicz differs from Dostoevsky in whose works this kind of humor is almost entirely absent. He is close, however, to Gogol in whom there is likewise a layer of meaning that can be described as comic extravaganza. For neither writer is it the most important layer; indeed, humor has been absent from many critical discussions of both writers. Yet without this comic undertone there would in a sense be no Gombrowicz.

The plots of the stories are fantastic. They contain false accounts of historical events and of the laws of thermodynamics, as well as absurd actions and situations. The hero of "Adventures" boasts of having devised a system which destroyed German defenses in 1918. In the same story, the Caspian Sea evaporates because a meteorite falls into it. In "Virginity" Alicia leaves her genteel home to rummage for bones in the

garbage can. In "Events on H.M.S. Banbury" sailors eat each
other's eyes. In "Premeditated Murder" the son not only confesses to murdering his father (who has died of a heart attack),
but also strangles the corpse so that the fingerprints on his
father's neck can serve as evidence of the "parricide." In "The
Memoir of Stefan Czarniecki" the husband-wife conflict assumes
monstrous proportions. In "Symposium at Countess Kotłubaj's"
the aristocrats dine on the body of a peasant boy from one of
their estates. Gombrowicz's stories do not refer to "real life"
as we know it from everyday experience. Unlike Chekhov,
Gombrowicz does not give us a sense of the flow of life, the almost tangible details of daily existence. He is not interested in
that. Nor is he interested in probing neurotic minds, although
a casual reading of his stories may produce that impression.
What fascinates him and what he presents with expertise is a
system of relations between individuals that manifests itself in
diverse actions and situations. He tries to reproduce this system
by means of bizarre chains of events.

As a result of this emphasis on a system of attitudes rather
than people and events, the protagonists of these stories tend
to be flat. They depict some human characteristic in an exaggerated way, seemingly to the exclusion of all others. Improbable
situations are the natural milieu of flat characters: Gombrowicz's
heroes would function poorly in realistic settings. Both in plot
structure and in character portrayal Gombrowicz follows non-
realistic methods. Not even in the early period of his writing
career did he try to imitate the nineteenth-century masters of the
realistic novel, as did so many Polish writers contemporary
with him.

In the system of human relations Gombrowicz presents, there
is very little sharing and a great deal of fighting. Gombrowicz's
characters view one another as competitors rather than fellow
humans. They play games with one another. Some do so without knowing the rules or even suspecting that such rules exist.
Others are skilled gamesmen whose every move is carefully
assessed beforehand. The reasons for playing are very strong
sado-masochistic drives among Gombrowicz's characters, desires
to subjugate others or be subjugated by them. "Dominate or be
dominated" is the motto of these characters. Like the Maids

in Jean Genet's play under this title, they are tossed to and fro between the need to worship and desecrate.

Gombrowicz's stories usually narrate a change of relationship: the person who was a dominating figure at the beginning usually is the subjugated one at the end. This basic plot structure assumes a variety of forms. It can be presented as the fight between aristocratic and plebeian instincts ("Symposium at Countess Kotłubaj's"). It can be a duel between the desire for refinement and for self-abasement ("On the Kitchen Stairs," "The Banquet"). It can be a neurotic oscillation between the love and hate of someone ("Kraykowski's Dancer"). Self-hatred can take the form of the desire to remake others into an image of oneself ("The Rat"). Fear of others and the unconscious desire to be the loser can take the form of fantastic adventures in which the hero is abused by others ("Adventures," "Events on H.M.S. Banbury"). Inability to sort out the reasons for love and hate of one's parents can result in the desire for universal destruction and an attempt to bring it about ("The Memoir of Stefan Czarniecki"). Sometimes the character's will to dominate is so strong it triumphs over the most adverse circumstances ("Premeditated Murder"). On the other hand, those dominated for a long time sometimes with unexpected force turn against their oppressors ("Virginity").

Thus a paradoxical situation arises. Gombrowicz's heroes are misanthropes, yet they exist only through their relation to others. Gombrowicz demonstrates that misanthropes need people more than others. The Dancer "comes alive" only when Kraykowski appears on the scene. Like Dostoevsky's "eternal husband," he is unable to generate enough self-respect to give up being dependent on someone he considers better than himself. Gombrowicz's characters depend on others in a negative way, their principal emotion being distrust and fear of their fellow human beings. They need stimuli to nourish and preserve their fears because the preservation of their very selves depends on it. In a masochistic way, they love those who mistreat them. The Dancer shoved aside by Kraykowski almost faints like a romantic heroine under the touch of her beloved. *"Ustanovka na drugogo"*—orientation toward the other—and a lack of true autonomy are the most characteristic features of the solitary and seemingly independent heroes of Gombrowicz's short stories.

What is the position of these stories in the totality of Gombrowicz's output? They are both dissimilar from, and very similar to, the rest of Gombrowicz's writing. First, the similarities. One striking feature of the stories is the intensity of tone. The narrator is always in earnest despite his use of rather formal language and suppression of any possible outburst of emotion. He re-experiences everything that is going on, one feels. Likewise, the I-narrator in the novels is also very close to the action he recounts. Although he conveys to us both the story and an assessment of it, the I-narrator's point of view remains in substantial agreement with the one he had when participating in the action.

Gombrowicz's narrators love artificiality. They speak and behave according to a code they have themselves devised, yet are as intense and passionate as the most pathetic romantic heroes. Part of their passion usually transforms into derision, however. Relentless and determined, they scorn all values, traditions, manners. This scorn sometimes has anti-nationalistic overtones. For instance, the protagonist's name in "The Memoir of Stefan Czarniecki" coincides with the name of the seventeenth-century military leader who became a national hero following his valiant defense of Poland against the Swedes. Czarniecki is mentioned in Sienkiewicz's *Trilogy*, and the strength of his reputation in the nation's memory has never diminished. With assumed casualness Gombrowicz presents as a namesake a cynical coward rather lacking in the noble ideals the average Polish reader associates with Czarniecki. The desire to break up stereotypes and develop a questioning attitude is apparent here. The same desire manifests itself in *Pornografia*, where Gombrowicz wrote about the war years in Poland, but instead of producing one more dirge or eulogy, probed the nature of lust and the conditions in which lust arises.

Though these stories are not inferior to the rest of Gombrowicz's works, they seem nevertheless to have been written by another person. Such an impression is created by differences in setting or the personalities of the narrators. First, the element of the exotic which looms larger in the stories, disappears from the longer narratives. Even when Gombrowicz describes in *Trans-Atlantic* and the *Journal*, relatively unfamiliar parts of the world such as South America, he "tames" these places by fitting them into categories of common experience. In the stories, every-thing said about these South Seas and aristocratic manors is deliberately made into something out-of-the-ordinary, remote, unavailable to the reader. Second, the autobiographical element is overtly present in the novels but only covertly in the stories. This is contrary to what happens in the works of most other writers. The narrators of these are more clearly distinguishable from their author than is the case with the novels' narrators. They are a bit affected, a trifle too eager to appear cold-blooded. They lack the naturalness of those down-to-earth raconteurs bearing Gombrowicz's own name in the novels.

Nothing is resolved in these stories—no solutions are even attempted. This state of affairs stems partly from the nature of the genre which does not admit of definitive conclusions. There exist, of course, many writers such as Henry James whose stories do convey a sense of distance necessary for comprehension of the events of the plot. A sense of reconciliation concludes many stories of Anton Chekhov. Not so in Gombrowicz. He plunges us *in medias res* without any introduction and leaves off without much explanation. This is an indication that the stories were written by a beginning author not yet ready to supply perspec-tive to his perception of life.

CHAPTER 3

Plays

GOMBROWICZ wrote three absurdist plays: *Ivona, Princess of Burgundia, The Marriage,* and *Operetta*. They are, perhaps, the best known of his works owing to stage productions. *Ivona, Princess of Burgundia* was written long before the theater of the absurd was heard of; *The Marriage* came out shortly before the period of popularity of Beckett and Ionesco; *Operetta* appeared after the Theater of the Absurd became literary history. This chronology indicates that in spite of technical similarities, one cannot speak of a direct relationship between Gombrowicz and the French theater of the 1950s.

One more play of Gombrowicz was recently discovered. Rescued from oblivion by Constantin Jeleński who found it among papers sent to him by the widow of the writer, the play entitled *Historia* is unfinished. It was published in *Kultura* in 1975. In the Foreword Jeleński points out that Gombrowicz alternated writing fiction and drama as follows:

1934–1935	*Ivona, Princess of Burgundia*
1935–1936	*Ferdydurke*
1944–1945	*The Marriage*
1948–1950	*Trans-Atlantic*
1951	*Historia*
1955–1957	*Pornografia*
1958	"Tandil" (the first version of *Operetta*)
1961–1962	*Cosmos*
1965–1966	*Operetta*[1]

I Structure

Written over a span of thirty years and at different stages of artistic development, Gombrowicz's dramas surprise us with

the abundance of features they have in common. The first of the
features we will mention is theatricality of atmosphere, setting,
and plot. Gombrowicz never allows us to forget we are in a
theater or that we are reading a piece for the theater. Nowhere
does he shun realistic convention so consistently as in his plays.
Rapid changes of place and time of action, stylized gestures
and words, plot sequences that do not belong to "real life"—all
these abound in his dramas. "Oh, for artificiality!" Gombrowicz
once exclaimed, a yearning he was to satisfy in creating his
works for the theater. Vsevolod Meierhold would have found
Gombrowicz's plays to his liking, since they lend themselves
more open to a producer's inventiveness than realistic plays. On
the other hand, Constantin Stanislavsky would have found Gombrowicz's dramaturgy impossible to deal with. Here the actor
is not supposed to identify with the role but rather act it in
such a way as to make the audience aware of the make-believe.
Not surprisingly, those producers who have staged Gombrowicz's
plays: Jorge Lavelli in Paris, Alf Sjöberg in Stockholm, Jerzy
Jarocki in Warsaw, are all descendants of Meierhold rather than
Stanislavsky.

While the time of action in the novels ranges from a few days
(*Pornografia, Cosmos*) to several months (*Ferdydurke, Trans-
Atlantic*), time tends to be ill-defined in the plays. *Operetta* and
Historia cover a period of many years. *The Marriage* ignores
the time dimension altogether, the action happening in a
dream. In *Princess Ivona,* time is vaguely defined. The tendency toward temporal looseness combined with the tendency toward instability of the place of action (we move from
France to Poland in *The Marriage,* and there are radical changes
in the scene of action owing to lapse of time in *Operetta*), echo
the romantic dramas of Słowacki, Mickiewicz and Krasiński
in which the temporal dimension was likewise vaguely defined.

Whereas in Gombrowicz's novels the action takes place in a
common, everyday world, in the plays we encounter a world
of royalty and aristocracy.[2] The setting is not, as has been the
case in the novels, middle class apartments and country houses
but royal castles and palaces. However, while the characters
are royalty and courtiers, they speak language not traditionally
suitable to their station. They use middle class and lower middle

class jargon for example. While this technique of mismatching a character with his speech is present in other works of Gombrowicz as well, it becomes here particularly noticeable owing to the centrality of dialogue. Likewise, gestures repeatedly are at odds with a character's station in life and his or her way of dressing. When the king in *Princess Ivona* hides behind a sofa and the king in *The Marriage* shows a lack of dignity in his behavior, a rare effect is achieved. Such actions bring Jarry's *King Ubu* to mind, but the similarity is only partial. While Jarry is all farce, there are sections in Gombrowicz's plays where the customary relationship between setting and dialogue is resumed, and the tone of the play becomes tragic instead of grotesque.

Partial similarities exist also between Gombrowicz and one of his predecessors in the Polish theater; Stanislaw Witkiewicz (1885-1939) who used a similar technique of combining the possible and the absurd in a plot. In Witkiewicz's plays, human encounters are but metaphors for psychological states rather than representations of real social encounters. Witkiewicz wrote his best plays in the 1920s when the reading public was not yet ready for his absurdist manner or preoccupation with man's metaphysical "insatiability" (the title of one of his novels). Some forty years later, he gained the reputation of being a brilliant, if elitist playwright. In the same period of time, Gombrowicz had become a well known figure also, a coincidence which contributed to the growth of general awareness concerning the common intuitions about the nature of their craft and possibilities for theater that these two writers share. From that time on, their names have been frequently associated.[3]

Indeed, the plays of Witkiewicz and Gombrowicz leave an impression that both men accept the assumption that theater should not divest itself of artificiality and that the actor should not try to make the spectator forget that he is looking at a stage—as opposed to "real life." Both playwrights play with the spectator's sense of logic and probability: there occur in their plays make-believe deaths (Witkiewicz's *The Water Hen* and Gombrowicz's *Operetta*) and characters who sometimes adopt a manner of speech or behavior incompatible with their station in life (Tadzio in *The Water Hen* and the King in *Princess*

Ivona). In some of their plays, we find a mixture of serious drama and operetta-like song (Witkiewicz's *The Shoemakers* and Gombrowicz's *Operetta*). It is possible to go on with this list of similarities.

However, in spite of these techniques of post-expressionist theater, Witkiewicz and Gombrowicz diverge at many essential points. The world views to which their plays give expression are incompatible. Witkiewicz's life passion was an investigation of man's metaphysical longing and inability to put up with limited possibilities for experiencing and understanding reality. Witkiewicz's characters are driven people, prone to melancholy and suicide, forever asking empty heaven for justice. The major concern of his plays is the inner life of characters seeking to satisfy their metaphysical longings in a godless universe.

In Gombrowicz, metaphysical concerns play no role at all. The world of his plays is a world of human relations: Gombrowicz is interested in how, when and why relationships change. What particularly fascinates him are the oscillations in social status and the insidious ways in which men acquire power over one another. His characters are social animals. In spite of their neuroses and introspective habits, they live in a world populated by real human beings. Witkiewicz's characters, on the other hand are asocial or antisocial. They either ignore or blame society for all the evils that befall them. Gombrowicz's characters exist *through* other characters. Thus despite similarities in both playwrights' approach to the theater and many coincidental convergences in their lives, they lead their readers and spectators toward profoundly different perceptions of the world.

As was the case with the short stories, there are recurrent plot patterns in Gombrowicz's plays. In the short stories the development consisted of a reversal of power: while at the beginning X wielded power over Y, at the end the relationship was reversed. In the plays, this simple sequence is enlarged. The three finished dramas have a tripartite structure which can be schematized as A—B—A$_1$. In addition to the first reversal, there occurs a second one which seems to put the players back in their original places. However, to see Gombrowicz's plays as circular means to view them with undue pessimism. There is in them a spiral movement, or cyclic revolution which rather than bringing

the characters to the same place in which they were at the
beginning, places them instead a notch beyond the initial place.
At the end, Gombrowicz's plays offer a bit of territory captured
from ignorance, a bit of freedom gained by man in his contest
with Form.

Let us now look at the three plays to see how this basic
pattern has been realized. First, *Princess Ivona*. At the beginning,
Ivona is the underdog, ridiculed and despised by everyone.
Gradually, her relation to others changes. At the court, she
controls others rather than being controlled by them. This cannot
be tolerated; she has to be put down and finally is. The resulting
reversal ends in the others exercising their "supremest" control
over her by murdering her. The crime is committed in spite of
the murderers having learned a great deal about themselves
only through Ivona's presence.

In *The Marriage*, the first occurring event of importance is
Henry's arrival at the home of his parents. He finds them powerless and humiliated, which also humiliates *him*. He devises a
plan by means of which he will gain power over others and
thus rid himself of the feeling of having been degraded. He first
tries an indirect approach by declaring his father king. This
fails. But Henry is much more successful in forcing his will
directly on others. He is unable, however, to remain in the
position of power, and voluntarily submits to others at the end.
Henry does this, however, from a position of self-knowledge
which he did not possess at the beginning. In *Operetta*, the two
reversals concern Albertine, a shopkeeper's daughter. At the
outset, she is free to dream of nakedness. But Prince Himalay
and Baron Firulet succeed in imposing their wishes on her: they
want to see her dressed, overdressed in fact, and they cover her
up with expensive clothing. Finally "conquered" when she appears at the Himalay ball wearing "a magnificent gown, boa,
gloves, necklace, parasol, muff, a hat in her hand," she is
placed on a platform as a symbol of high fashion—and her
enslavement to it. A complicated denouement frees her from
the impositions of aristocratic society. At the end, Albertine rises
from the coffin, all naked as she once dreamed to be, free again.
The Form which her adversaries had so devotedly cultivated,

therefore, is in ruin. They acknowledge her ascendancy proclaiming their mistakes and final defeat.

The Marriage and *Operetta*, the two plays of Gombrowicz written in his mature years, contain a development in which self-knowledge becomes a privilege of the defeated. Not absolute and perfect, the kind of wisdom which Herman Hesse's heroes achieve, it is only a notch above the preceding ignorance. But self-knowledge nonetheless, is there, and given to those who in some way lose their illusions about the advantages of winning "the duel of wills." Therefore I cannot agree with Lucien Goldmann's statement that *Operetta* represents a radical departure from earlier dramas.[4] It is true that emphasis here is placed on the necessity for immaturity, but the characters arrive at a realization of this by the same route Henry takes in shedding his illusions concerning his ability to sustain the pressure and loneliness of power.

Gombrowicz is then a playwright with a message. Like it or not he cannot entirely avoid being part of Polish literature which traditionally has been favorably inclined to "messages." Here again Gombrowicz differs from Alfred Jarry and S. I. Witkiewicz, the two writers whom he occasionally resembles. Unlike these two, he is more inclined to look for remedies and to urge his reader to put them into practice. Gombrowicz's messages, however, are not delivered by prophets but by clowns and people with suspect reputations. They blatantly admit their lack of competence and their condition of being "honeycombed by childishness." Gombrowicz's prophets mock their own pronouncements. An appearance of dignity is not what Gombrowicz seeks. Dignity for him is always a put-on which he never allows to become characteristic of any of his characters—or of his own writing style.

II   Ivona, Princess of Burgundia: *The Psychology of Shame*

In 1935, *Ivona, Princess of Burgundia* appeared in the literary monthly *Skamander*. The event passed almost unnoticed. No theater in Poland produced the play, and the author himself forgot about it in the difficult war years. Twenty years later a theater in Cracow staged *Ivona* and the play turned out to be a huge success. In the 1950s and 1960s *Ivona* was produced many times in Poland and in western Europe, and was readily accepted by most audiences to which it was shown. Some critics compared it to the plays of the French absurdists. The similarities, however, are misleading. While the Theater of the Absurd dwells on the emptiness of modern life and the incomprehensibility of the universe, *Ivona* has no metaphysical concerns. It deals instead with practical living, the here and now of daily human activities. It flaunts its indifference to philosophical concerns of a Beckett or an Ionesco.

The plot of *Ivona* like all Gombrowicz's plots is preposterous. A dull-looking and timid girl named Ivona meets the crown prince Philip. Unexpectedly, the prince decides to marry her. Presented to the king and the queen, Ivona begins to attend court functions. People laugh at her and marvel that Philip wants to marry her. Soon the laughter dies away and another feeling creeps in. The royal family and the courtiers begin to be disturbed by Ivona's presence, her perpetual silence and apparent unconcern for the niceties of social life. A certain kind of behavior is expected from her, since now *she has* a place in the web of social relationships. But, wittingly or unwittingly, she ignores matters to which others routinely take heed. People begin to feel uncomfortable in her presence. When she appears, the customary social exchanges are disturbed. Her presence undermines the social structure in which the rest of the characters who play games with one another rather than engage in genuine human contact live. In such a situation, when one player suddenly stops playing, the whole system collapses. Ivona is this non-playing player, and the confusion she causes is universal.

As the play progresses, it becomes increasingly clear that Ivona is not just a timid girl. At first she appears clumsy and passive, which attracts others as clumsiness often attracts people looking for entertainment. But once attracted, the onlookers are caught like flies on flypaper. Despite her timidity Ivona turns out to be self-contained and independent of others whom she does not try to impress. This lack of concern irritates, angers and makes them hostile and aggressive toward Ivona. But their anger does not free them from her presence; on the contrary, it makes this presence even more acutely felt. On one of the infrequent occasions when Ivona speaks up, she says: "It is a wheel, it goes round and round in circles. . . . It goes round and round, always, everybody, everything." She does not understand her mysterious power, but is aware of it. There is some "lethargic wisdom" in her, as Prince Philip remarks. "You . . . you realist!" he shouts at her toward the end of the play.

Ivona makes the courtiers and the royal family uncomfortable because she does not play the social game. As the game breaks down, other more profound reasons for her being found so irritating emerge. She immobilizes other characters' social selves, exposing inner selves which they carefully guard from the gazes of those around them. Prince Philip feels that Ivona's indifference is a way of pointing out that he is not the forceful and decisive person he should be as the crown prince. The courtiers detect in Ivona's behavior an allusion to their own secret defects. They also see the royal engagement as a way to show them up. The maids of honor, for example, suddenly remember that they wear wigs and false teeth. The queen fears that the mawkish poetry she writes has been found out. The king and his chamberlain begin to talk about the seamstress who had committed suicide after the king seduced her with the help of the chamberlain. They all remember things which they usually conceal from others. Ivona causes such serious discomfort, that she has to be got rid of. Plans to do away with her begin to germinate in everyone's mind. The murder proceeds according to the chamberlain's plan. He suggests that pike be served at a banquet honoring Ivona. If the affair is handled properly, he feels, she should choke on a fishbone.

Who is Ivona? She makes others aware of their shortcomings, but is not herself a moralistic character. She has nothing in common with the self-righteous Alcestes and Chatskys of world literature. She is not a saint either. Her ability to make others aware of their inner selves has nothing in common with Tikhon's ability to extract a confession from Stavrogin. Like the imaginary adversaries in Kafka's stories Ivona is faceless, a device rather than a character;[5] she personifies those situations and circumstances in which we look at others without having prepared "a face to meet the faces that we meet." She

is a catalyzer of the fear of scorn and ridicule. Gombrowicz's
play argues that this seemingly infantile fear is latent even in
mature personalities. In traditional language, this fear used to be
called shame. I say "used to" because for a long time, shame
was not a feeling which psychologists liked to discuss. According to Erik Erikson, shame is "early and easily absorbed by
guilt."[6] Guilt has been a focus of attention of psychologists and
literary critics alike during the past decades. It plays a major
role in Freudian theory, and its recognition largely accounts
for the popularity of such writers as Kafka whose works explore
the state of feeling guilty.

Some researchers, however, view shame as distinct and
independent of guilt in the Freudian sense. In *Shame and Guilt,*
Gerhart Piers and Milton Singer point out that, "Whereas guilt
is generated whenever a boundary is touched or transgressed,
shame occurs when a goal is not being reached. It thus indicates
a real 'shortcoming.' "[7] And the threat implied in shame anxiety
"is abandonment, and not mutilation (castration) as in guilt."
In *On Shame and the Search for Identity* Helen Lynd maintains
that shame involves exposure, especially an exposure which is
unexpected or one which we are unable to prevent.[8] These
researchers conceptualize something implicit in Gombrowicz's
play. The characters become increasingly uncomfortable as
Ivona's gaze makes them realize that in some way they fall
short of the "ideal" and that this fact is becoming obvious to
those around them. Her adversaries resolve to avoid final exposure by destroying Ivona. Before this happens, however, they
adopt half-measures to hide their secret characteristics.

Gombrowicz very skillfully presents the range of possibilities
which the characters have available to keep their immaturity and
shortcomings well hidden. Ivona's aunts try to hide their shame
of her lack of conventional success by endlessly repeating that
they have done everything possible to make Ivona successful
and to marry her off to a suitable young man. Prince Philip is
ashamed of the insecurity he experiences in Ivona's presence.
In order to circumvent it, he decides to marry her, since as his
wife she will depend on him and not he on her. Like king
Gnulo in "The Banquet" he lacks regal feelings, and cannot
bear the appearance of a person more self-contained than he.

The queen tries to master her shame by exaggerating her royal behavior. She is uneasy because Ivona exposes her secret longing for "suppleness" and "floppiness." From that point on, the queen's foremost concern in her daily dealings with others will be to maintain an austere and dignified pose. The king feels that since others may regard him as a reprehensible character, he must respond by being aggressive and shouting at Ivona: "I am not a beast, I do not eat little children, I am not an ogre!" The maids of honor believe that their attempts to beautify themselves have become obvious to others. Afraid of being found out and put to shame, they affect scorn toward Ivona as a preventive measure.

Shame is unacceptable in the society Gombrowicz presents. Here everything functions in accordance with the false identities assumed by the characters. When these identities are exposed or threatened to be exposed as masks, the characters feel panicky and cannot perform their social roles. The social game has to go on; its collapse would involve too many risks for each of the players. Ivona, "the universal irritant," must die.

The world of *Princess Ivona* consists of people who have adopted masks of maturity for the sake of others and thus prove themselves profoundly dependent on the way others perceive them. They stand ready to do anything to maintain a semblance of maturity. In the play, after a temporary upset, they succeed—but, as Gombrowicz's later works show, this can only be a temporary success.

III   The Marriage: *The Divorce Between Meaning and Event*

Gombrowicz's second and most important play is *The Marriage* (Ślub). It was written in the years of poverty and uncertainty in Argentina when his position as a writer was at its most precarious. About the circumstances in which the play came into being he says the following:

I had started *The Marriage* during the war. It gradually grew inside me, in fits and starts, during my stay in the Argentine, day by day. *Faust* and *Hamlet* were my models, but only because of their quality of genius. I wanted to write a "great" play, a "work of genius," and I went back to those works which I had read with veneration

in my youth. And my ambitions were accompanied by a certain cunning. I sensed slyly that it was easier to write a "great" work than
simply a "good" work. The paths of genius seemed less arduous
to me.[9]

Gombrowicz expresses here an idea similar to one which
pervades his play: for a person with a sufficient amount of
creative energy it is easier to strike new paths than to follow
in someone else's footsteps. Or, it is easier to generate an event,
to make things happen, and let the meaning arise when new
facts have already been established, than start with a given
meaning and tailor events according to *its* demands. Meanings
are but products of will; the only reality is the event. It is
therefore important to affect the course of action, and then, by
a relatively small effort of the will, achieve meaning which will
glorify this will.

The Marriage is a parody of three rituals: the wedding ceremony; the annointing of the king; and the homage paid by a
son to his father. The first two parodies come into being through
the will power of Henry, a Polish soldier in France during
World War II; the third is willed by the author himself. The
parodies arise by means of a reversal in the customary relation
between man and ritual. The rule of any ritual is that men
submit to it; they let the ritual possess them rather than they
trying to master it. This submission of human will to the
meaning of an event does not exist in *The Marriage,* where
Henry is seen to establish his own rituals—"like Stalin or Hitler,"
to quote Gombrowicz's commentary on the play. The author
"wills" to pit the son against the father or—by metaphorical
extension—sons against their fatherland.

The dream technique is adopted to bring all these parodies
together. Henry dreams he has returned to his home in Poland
to find his aristocratic family changed into innkeepers, and his
fiancée Molly transformed into a barmaid. To restore his parents'
dignity and his fiancée's virginity, Henry begins to treat them
with the respect due to royalty and declares his father "king."
But the drunkards in the inn succeed in sowing discord between
his father and him. A fight ensues. Henry hesitates in deciding
which side to take before finally declaring himself king and

making plans to marry Molly. He intends to be both bridegroom and priest at the wedding ceremony, having come to the conclusion that in the world in which he lives, "Holiness, majesty, power, law, morality, love, ridiculousness, stupidity, wisdom—all these come from people in the same way that vodka comes from potatoes" (V, 119).

The qualities ascribed to people are a consequence of the conduct of others rather than an integral part of those assumed to possess them. Dignity and distinction seem "pumped" into one like hot air into a balloon. Meanings ascribed to rituals are detachable from them. Rituals are series of actions performed by human beings to which meanings may be attached by individuals capable of doing so. In a world without meaning, those who understand the possibility of enacting rituals and assigning them meaning by an act of creative *fiat* are going to end up being the winners.

Henry is such a person. Having dethroned his father, he now thinks of getting rid of his friend Johnny whom he suspects of having a liaison with Molly. At Henry's suggestion—which contains a veiled threat—Johnny commits suicide. Henry the king is now ready to be both the celebrant and the participant in his own marriage. At the last moment, however, he fails and betrays his own rules of behavior. It appears that his will is too weak and it cannot withstand the pressure of always forcing its meaning on others. Henry turns out to be incapable of treating his friend's death as if it were merely another opportunity for his will to supply an event with meaning. Meaning here seems rather to arise of itself and it defeats Henry. He does not suffer remorse in the traditional sense: that would be a slick moralistic ending for which Gombrowicz is too profound an artist. Henry feels that some kind of symmetry has been violated, and, in order to restore it, orders his guards to arrest him. He had, in a sense already been "imprisoned" by the symmetry before actually becoming a prisoner in the physical sense. Henry appears to belong to some incomprehensible order. When this order claims him, he must follow, abandoning those who had been so crucial to his former plans: his mother, his courtiers, his enemies—the other people.

Echoes of existential thought pervade the play. Henry's

attempts to give a new meaning to his parents' plight is one
instance. His realization that he is after all free to marry Molly
and to treat her as if she were a queen is another. In Henry's
world, all the altars are built by men to worship men's ideas
rather than those of divine origin. In the preface to the play
Gombrowicz says: "Man is subject to that which is created
'between' individuals and has no other divinity but that which
springs from other people." While this wide-ranging freedom is
openly acknowledged, its consequences remain ambiguous.
Henry fails. But, is it a superman's failure to be superman, or
a realization that man for some reason cannot exert his will and
creativity indefinitely? "It is not we who say words but words
which say us," says Henry. Is the whole idea of supermanhood an
illusion, a futile attempt to escape the symmetries of the system?
The only "revelation" the author affords us is the statement that
Henry's marriage never takes place.

Henry who has enacted a mock ritual by declaring his father
king intends to enact another by marrying Molly. These two
make-believe rituals are expressly described in the play; Henry
speaks about them to himself and to others. The play, however,
implicitly parodies yet another ritual, or series of rituals in
which sons pay homage to their fathers or—more broadly,
people express allegiance to their fatherland. An explicit parody
of such rituals occurs in *Trans-Atlantic,* the novel Gombrowicz
wrote after he completed *The Marriage.* In both works the
parody is accomplished by combining the Freudian motif of the
father-son rivalry with irreverent use of quotations from those
Polish authors who have been the mainstays of Polish patriotic
tradition.

In spite of Henry's initial attempt to restore his father's position
of superiority, the father fears him. He does not want to be
"touched" by his son or by the Drunkard who is spokesman for
Henry's intuitions about the possibilities of human will. The
father will eventually be imprisoned by the son, the Oedipal
threat fulfilled. In conducting the plot this way Gombrowicz
gives expression to a belief that the values of traditional patriotism (very strong in Poland in his time) should not be immune
to questioning. Why should one submit oneself to the father
—or the fatherland? What about the "sonland" (Gombrowicz

coined this word in *Trans-Atlantic*) which we, the sons, inhabit?

To emphasize Henry's realization that all values and meanings are arbitrary, Gombrowicz in the play blends together several kinds of contemporary Polish: the speech of the educated classes, peasant dialect, city jargon, and turns of phrase borrowed from well known works of Polish Romanticism and the Renaissance. He makes Henry's parents and the Drunkard switch from one style of speech to another thereby underscoring the artificiality and flimsiness of social categories based on manners and verbal refinement. When Henry's father and mother speak to him in a peasant dialect, it is obvious that the only thing which formerly separated them from the peasants was the language they used. The poets Mickiewicz, Słowacki and Kochanowski are quoted out of context (V, 126; V, 123; V, 129) for similar reasons. When amidst phrases of a lower middle class conversation there sounds a solemn phrase from a romantic play, the latent false romantic pathos is readily exposed.

In the contemporary context, Gombrowicz's probing of the structure of authority extends to experiences consequent to membership in a particular majority or minority group. *The Marriage* brings its principal character to a realization that the problem of being in a minority extends far beyond those social and political rights which can be legislated. Its unlegislated realm is the realm of "Form"—the same Form from which the hero of *Ferdydurke* had tried to escape and of which Gombrowicz likes to speak in commentaries to his works. Men force Form on one another; they ritualize and give meaning to their own set of trivia. Being in a minority means that the war over trivia has already been lost, that one's small psychological habits have been rejected and disapproved of by others. A minority person has the power to act, but is powerless to assign meaning to his actions, as that is done by others. In the preface to the play Gombrowicz says: "If in a play by Shakespeare, for instance, someone cried at his father: 'You pig!' the dramatic effect would depend upon the fact that a son was insulting his father; but when that occurs in this play, the drama takes place between the person who cries and his own cry. His cry may assume a positive or a negative character; it may exalt the person who uttered it or, on the contrary, it may thrust him

into an abyss of shame and disapprobation."[10] The conflict between authority (fathers, fatherlands, majorities) and a lack of
it (sons, "sonlands," minorities) takes place not only in the realm
of physical coercion but also, and primarily in the realm of
Form created by men whose vision is blurred and who alternate
between a submission to the symmetries of the system and a
desire to exercise the force of their wills.

The omnipresence of Form and man's freely exercised ability
to give the particular significance to events he wishes them to
have are the two essential ingredients of Gombrowicz's play.
On the most essential level, *The Marriage* enacts a confrontation
between these two. Form, symbolized at the end by the stately
rhythm of the funeral march, seems to prevail; the play as a
whole demonstrates, however, that Form is closely related to
the will and its triumph cannot but bring about another upsurge
of will. This dialectic is Gombrowicz's answer to those existen-
talist and pre-existentialist philosophers (Sartre, Nietzsche,
Schopenhauer) whom he followed part way but from whom he
eventually diverged, voicing his own vision of the human
predicament.

IV   Historia: *Witold Gombrowicz Faces Himself*

The very title of this unfinished play is laden with ambiguity.
Historia in Polish means both "history" and "story." The play,
which begins as a family chronicle with Witold, his parents and
siblings conversing with one another, appears at its end to be
a historical drama. It is the only work of Gombrowicz which
draws directly on personal biography. It is also the only work
where political events of Gombrowicz's time play a considerable
role. The members of Gombrowicz's family double-deal with
one another. They wear a "face" even within the family circle,
enslaved by their Form. Political implications of wearing a "face"
are sketched out in the rest of the play. Both parts of it contain
the figure of Witold dashing back and forth with his message
about Form and its many prisons.

In act one, members of the Gombrowicz family disapprove
of Witold's bare feet and give reasons why he should put on
shoes. The mother fears bacteria and dirt which her son may

pick up while going barefooted. His brother Janusz accuses him
of trying to ingratiate himself with the servants. Another brother
Jerzy blames him for his lack of refinement. His father reproaches
him for not observing the customs; his sister Rena, for consciously annoying Mother and Father. Soon the family changes
into an examination committee which will decide whether
Witold should receive the maturity certificate. To help the
examinee overcome his timidity, they all take their shoes off.
As soon as this happens, their personalities change. Instead of
their "faces," we now see their hidden selves and learn something
about their motivation processes. The questions change accordingly. Mother asks Witold whether he is capable of being
as cowardly and hypocritical as she; Father, whether he could
live like a model citizen if his income were fifty thousand złotys
a year. Rena inquires whether he would be able to persuade
himself to believe in God who does not exist; Jerzy, whether
he knows how to be superficial and consciously avoid deep com-
mitments. Witold answers "yes" to all questions. Members of
the examining committee congratulate him: he has passed the
examination and will receive a certificate of *immaturity*.

In act two Witold becomes secret envoy of Tsar Nicholas II
to Emperor Wilhelm II. Upon arriving barefoot at the court
of Emperor Wilhelm, he insists on speaking to the Emperor in
private. The rest of the act is missing. On the basis of unpublished notes, Jeleński suggests that Witold's advice to Wilhelm
was to flee from his empire in order to be rid of the image of
himself as Emperor perpetuated by his subjects.

Act three takes place in the 1930s. Witold and his fellow
writers drink coffee in a Warsaw coffee shop. Marshal Piłsudski
occupies the table next to theirs. He orders Witold to go to
Berlin and propose a nonagression treaty to Hitler. Witold
assures him that Hitler does not exist; this makes Piłsudski
angry.

The play appears to be a collection of random fragments.
Times and people in it change with a rapidity characteristic
of the historical dramas of Polish Romanticism rather than that
of the modern theater. Even in its present incomplete form,
however, the play recognizably belongs to the Polish literary
tradition, which it parodies. Just as *Trans-Atlantic* is a parody

of the Polish romantic epic *Pan Tadeusz*, *Historia* is a mock heroic version of the Polish romantic dramas *Forefathers' Eve* (*Dziady*) by Adam Mickiewicz and *Kordian* by Juliusz Słowacki. These authors had been targets of Gombrowicz's sarcasm ever since *Ferdydurke*. The episodic technique of *Historia* and the lack of continuity in its plot resemble *Forefathers' Eve*, since part one of the latter consists of unfinished fragments, while part three is a play in itself. Witold, Konrad and Kordian are all possessed by an *idée fixe*. The two romantic characters undertake to free Poland and all humanity from the tyranny of the Russian tsar. Amidst tragic rhetoric, they fail. Witold also feels that history has gone berserk and that he is destined to improve matters. He offers advice to Emperor Wilhelm, Marshal Piłsudski and Tsar Nicholas that they dare to throw away clothes and pretense—go barefoot—be average—stop pretending they are made for the extremes of temperature because in fact they belong to the moderate climate. Witold is himself, of course, a Konrad or a Kordian in clownish disguise, a mock hero and self-deflating pundit. He does not plan to assassinate anyone; instead, he advises the European rulers to assassinate the Form surrounding them.

To give artistic shape to Witold's outlook on politics would have been a tremendous achievement. It is possible that Gombrowicz felt unfit for his task and therefore left *Historia* unfinished.

Witold's outlook deserves discussion because it throws light on Gombrowicz's development as a writer. Witold believes that if people only realized that those wielding power are in fact as fragile and powerless as those around them, there would have been no Hitlers or Stalins. For Hitler or Stalin to exist, there must be others who elevate him to the height of his authority. Paradoxically, power wielding personalities are more dependent on others than the powerless. Is it possible ever to go barefoot and return to sanity by throwing off one's clothes? The thirty-three year old author of *Ferdydurke* did not think so; the forty-eight year old author of *Historia* says that it is worth trying.

In *Historia* Gombrowicz turns out to be a writer with an ax to grind, a task to perform. Much as he would have disliked to see himself so described, the fact remains that his alter ego Witold is a man of a single purpose. Whenever adulation of some suspect authority takes place, Witold exclaims that the king is naked. Openly and explicitly, he champions immaturity in public and private life. The play might be read as a statement to himself about the actual scope of his undertaking. The autobiographical tone prevalent in *Historia* is, perhaps, one reason why Gombrowicz never spoke about the play to anyone and why he preserved it among his papers even while habitually destroying his first drafts. ,*Historia* might be a story Gombrowicz told only to himself. It is autobiographical not because the members of Gombrowicz's family appear in it but because it speaks explicitly of his belief about the common disease which is the public and private self and of the medication which must be taken to cure it.

V Operetta: *Creative Immaturity*

Operetta (*Operetka*) parodies the genre to which it purports to belong. The genre of operetta is in itself a parody of serious dramatic performance. Gombrowicz's play, therefore, a parody of a parody twice removed from outward seriousness shares, in the words of its author, the "divinely idiotic and perfectly sclerotic" quality of the genre by which it is inspired. Gombrowicz tried to make this play as entertaining as possible. In his stage directions, he recommended that popular tunes from old Viennese operettas be used as accompaniments to the monologues. Some characters are supposed to dance and sing their parts. As a result, *Operetta* is an "easier" play than *The Marriage*. Its soapy love story, absurd high society setting and happy ending generate an atmosphere apparently conducive to carefree entertainment. Behind this façade, however, the play sums up Gombrowicz's intuitions about the role of immaturity in history.

The three-tiered plot parodies the three traditional elements of the operetta genre: a love story that ends happily; an obstacle course which the lovers must surmount; a highly schematized and simplified picture of social life and manners. The love story begins in a conventional way. Prince Himalay is interested in Albertine, a shopkeeper's daughter. As a member of high society, he has no opportunity to become acquainted with her, the two frequenting entirely different social circles. The process of their becoming acquainted parodies the usual soapy plot of operettas. In order to meet Albertine, the prince hires a pickpocket to steal Albertine's pendant. He plans to appear at the moment when Albertine notices the pendant is missing, tell her about the theft, and hand the pendant back to her. While no sooner thought than done, the results of this successful scheme lead the plot further and further away from the customary operettic treatment of incipient love. The pendant is stolen while Albertine is asleep on a park bench. In her sleep, she feels the touch of the thief's hand on her bare bosom, and upon awakening expresses far more interest in the thief and nakedness, than in Prince Himalay and the expensive clothes he offers her. The love story, then, does not really come off. Instead, a typical Gombrowicz conflict between clothes and nakedness, Form and formlessness arises.

The obstacle course which assumes the form of revolutions and wars becomes increasingly irrelevant to the pair of lovers.

The three acts of *Operetta* extend over a period of forty years, from the time preceding World War I to the end of World War II. At first, the differences between the haves and the have-nots are presented in a schematized way: the haves perform their monotonous rituals epitomized in meaningless conversations ("Prince. Me? Say something? (cautiously) Gooa, gooa? Marchioness. Gloogloogloot! Banker. Ploot plat!") and in the recurring phrase "Lord Blotton's chairs . . . Lord Blotton's chairs . . ." The have-nots are represented by the servants at the Himalay estate. Onstage, they clean and polish their masters' shoes. Revolution, a predictable outcome, wipes out the Himalay castle, as well as the prince's family and friends, even though it is one of the taboo subjects of the bourgeois genre of the operetta and "cannot" take place in stable operetta society. Gombrowicz's parody thus reaches its peak when he evokes a vision of a certain dramatic society by presenting us with its opposite. In this respect, then, *Operetta* resembles Brecht's *Threepenny Opera*.

The third tier of the plot concerns the Master of fashion Fior who is invited to a grand ball at the Himalay castle. Like the ancient Greek chorus, Fior comments on events rather than participating in them. Since he is a fashion designer, his commentary concerns the changes in fashions and the reasons for them. Fior understands that the changes in clothing styles do not depend on the whims of a designer but rather on "the winds of history." In other words, he understands that the change in one signifier depends on the changes in others, for only in such a way can the balances of the system be preserved. The *how* of these changes Fior is unable to analyze. He needs the intuitions of those he is supposed to dress up in order to devise new dressing conventions. Therefore, he will attend a masked ball during which the guests will wear the costumes of their choice covered by sackcloth. Toward the end of the ball, the sackcloth will be removed and thus, what people want and expect, or "the winds of history," will be revealed.

We find in *Operetta,* then, a symbolization of the pretenses of high society and an indication that this empty and insipid world is very rigorously structured.

Operetta yields itself badly to summary. Like many post-expressionist plays, it consists of a series of rapidly changing scenes which truly work only on the stage with music and dance accompanying the dialogue. In his commentary Gombrowicz says that modern plays resemble musical scores in that they come alive only in performance. On paper, they remain obscure outlines. He felt that of all his plays *Operetta* was the one which needed the stage most.

Operetta, a commentary on history, in Gombrowicz's phrase, "a proclamation of the bancrupcy of all political ideology," can—and has been—interpreted as rightist *or* leftist, depending on the sympathies of the critic. Perhaps the best known of the political interpretations is that of Lucien Goldmann who sees *Operetta* as an expression of Gombrowicz's political optimism, a play with a, positive hero, a statement of hope about the course of human history. More particularly, he sees in *Operetta* (1967) a forecast of the events of May, 1968 in France,[12] at which time, the young people of Paris organized meetings and demonstrations to proclaim their "rejection of the values of the old society" and "the hope that a truly human world may yet come about." They rejected the Stalinist revolutionaries (represented in the

play by the butler Joseph, alias Count Hufnagel) as well as the
old ruling classes (Prince Himalay).

Goldmann's argument does not take into account that the 1968
events were an expression of an ideology—however vaguely
formulated by the participants—even though directed against
most right wing and left wing ideologies. But *Operetta* opposes
all ideology, and shifts the conflict from the sphere of interest
literature shares with sociology and political theory, to one it
shares with psychology. The conflict in *Operetta* is between
desire for maturity and desire for immaturity; between Form
and formlessness; clothes and nakedness. The plot in which
social groups are included is but a metonym for the conflict
between an individual and the Form he generates, or between
his Form and the Form coming from another source.

The play presents Gombrowicz's view of the disastrous consequences of captivity by one's own Form. Those characters who
chose to ritualize their Form become its slaves. In the plot
this is presented as a degeneration of the ideals which the
characters nominally support. The aristocrats of *Operetta* have
degenerated into snobs. Their major concern in life is to make
an impression on others, both their peers and their lackeys. The
theorist of revolution is a masochist convinced of his own un-
worthiness and craving punishment from his inferiors, a twentieth-century version of Russia's "repentant nobleman" of the
nineteenth century. Joseph, the revolutionary, is a barbarian and
fool mouthing the professor's phrases and blindly following a
desire for revenge and violent action. The Catholic priest has
degenerated into a defender of the status quo. Fior, the puppet
master of this grotesque theater, perceives the real state of affairs
behind the masquerade but himself is unable and unwilling to
act. Following desires for maturity, all these characters had
adopted certain sets of beliefs and attitudes with which they
identified—with disastrous results. For human beings to adopt
a pretense of maturity means they become prisoners of Form.
We run the danger of becoming enslaved to something we once
might have said or to the way we once behaved. But every self-
expression is "deformed" by the "other." When we treat it as
if it were *not* subject to deformation, we become entrenched
in falsity which inevitably leads to the degeneration in us of

ideals we once embraced. Human beings who incessantly follow a desire for maturity end up exhibiting the sterile pretenses of the Himalays or the sterile viciousness of revolutionaries. In the long run sterility is unbearable; its reign inevitably ends in general destruction, "the wriggling heap" of *Ferdydurke* (to be discussed in chapter four).

The end of the play contains a scene of such general destruction. The characters meet in the ruins of the Himalay castle. Having lost their previous aspirations and assumptions about the world, they seek to bury their former convictions in a coffin (which conveniently appears carried by two gravediggers). Both the haves and have-nots deposit their former beliefs in the coffin. The last to do so is Master Fior who curses man's clothing, "those bloodstained masks that eat into our bodies," the Form man created for his own undoing. When the grim ceremony is almost over, there comes a surprise. Albertine, the girl who loved nakedness, rises from the coffin and proclaims the victory of nakedness. Her appearance rejuvenates all present. Full of joy and energy, they begin to dance and sing.

Who is Abertine and what is her role in the maturity-immaturity dialectic? She is the shopkeeper's daughter, a person of limited horizons (she hardly ever says or does anything), an archetypal pinup girl who had been rescued from impending death in the Himalay castle by two pickpockets. These three are altogether unwise, inarticulate, and, by the profession of the pickpockets associated with the "refuse rooms" of human minds. Their appearance, however, becomes a source of joy for all. The same characters who moments earlier were resigned, desperate and miserable are now transformed into lively human beings who stand ready to experience and explore life once more. The same immaturity they once rejected in favor of "adult" attitudes, blossoms forth its generative and creative powers. Albertine's young and unadorned body is admired by all. She represents the charm of things whose potential has not yet been realized, and is the source of the rapture which man requires to exist. Such needs were previously hidden behind a façade of wisdom, whether worldly or other-worldly. Now that all façades have been destroyed, the characters feel free to give expression to their real needs. They previously felt uncomfortable with immaturity—now they openly acknowledge its rejuvenating charms. They do so in spite of Albertine's having been saved for them by two pickpockets—an embarrassing situation, considering that these "rejuvenated" characters belong to a very different social group either by virtue of their background (the Princes Himalay) or the seriousness of their concerns (the Professor and the revolutionaries). The play ends with the pickpockets taking credit for the saving of Albertine: "It was us! It was us!," they keep repeating. Thus, Albertine's vital charm and the petty vice of the pickpockets are inextricably connected.

The inevitability of this linkage is *Operetta's* final discovery. Human beings need the charm of immaturity in order to live, even though immaturity is also characterized by qualities we would rather not acknowledge openly. Immaturity means imperfection. Yet human beings strive for perfection. The drive for perfection, however, often produces a sterility which cannot sustain them in the long run. The *sustaining* quality resides in *immaturity,* in open acknowledgment that "everything is honeycombed with childishness." Immaturity is many things we do not want to be, but it also is a source of our strength and creativity. If we want the second, we must accept the first. If we want Albertine, we must accept the fact that she has been rescued by the pickpockets. The alternatives lead to the abandonment of hope and to the mournful celebration of the sort the characters had participated in before Albertine appeared among them. In *Operetta,* the conflict between maturity and immaturity is shown to contain the elements of the conflict between life and death.

CHAPTER 4

Novels

I *Structure*

THE four novels: *Ferdydurke, Trans-Atlantic, Pornografia,* and *Cosmos,*[1] are first person narratives whose narrator actively participates in the plot. He also stands provocatively close to the author: he is called "Witold" in *Pornografia, Cosmos* and, occasionally, in *Ferdydurke,* and "Mr. Gombrowicz" in *Trans-Atlantic.* In *Ferdydurke* and *Trans-Atlantic* his age, profession and circumstances of life resemble Gombrowicz's. The narrator must not, of course, be totally identified with the author in spite of the similarities. The name the narrator bears, for example, is a way of teasing the reader; it is an inversion of the device used by many writers who stimulate the readers' curiosity by saying that "all events and persons in this book are fictitious." This naturally makes the reader suspect the opposite. The writer's coquettish assurances that the world of the novel and the author's life have nothing in common, are never taken too seriously by the reader. This does not mean that readers as a rule confuse the main character in the story with the writer; it does mean, however, that they recognize that the ambiance surrounding a central hero is usually closely related to the author's vision of life. With assumed indifference to custom Gombrowicz stresses this by giving his heroes his own name.

There is another curious regularity in Gombrowicz's novels: beside the narrator stands another character, an alter ego and helper playing a greater role in the plot than the narrator himself.[2] He generates the plot by conceiving a plan of action which he and the narrator follow and is superior to the narrator in many ways. He is the most intelligent character in the novel, may be more experienced than the narrator (Frederick in *Pornografia*), more exotic (Gonzalez in *Trans-Atlantic*), more energetic (Mientus in *Ferdydurke*), or more mysterious (Leo in *Cosmos*). He is quoted often enough to provide the reader with direct knowledge of him. In comparison to him, the narrator's figure and voice pale and become insignificant.

Owing to the two figures of narrator and friend, Gombrowicz's novels present the following case from the point of view of the narrative method: the narrator relates what happens and describes his friend "the stage producer"; he also gives an evaluation of events and his friend. At the same time, the friend's voice is heard often enough for the reader to form an independent opinion of what the motivation and understanding of the friend are. The "stage producer" often has a deeper understanding of what is being discussed than the narrator, something the author obviously plans. A narrator as knowledgeable as the author—or the ideal reader for that matter—is a device of romantic rather than post-realistic prose. He would be an uncomfortable character for a twentieth-century writer to handle: the amount of explicitness he would have to engage in would be more than reticent and word-conscious contemporary prose could bear. Accordingly, Gombrowicz's "Mr. Gombrowicz" tells us the story in a moderately perceptive way. The author allows us to fill in narrative gaps by looking toward the stage producer for additional explanations. The reader's final judgment is arrived at by a juxtaposing of these two voices and assessing their relative importance. The ultimate meaning of the events is thus left for the reader to figure out. The stage producers occasionally hint at it, but never attempt to explain it fully.

Each of the narrators of Gombrowicz's novels is more laconic than the last. Johnnie in *Ferdydurke* still engages in long monologues on Form, the mug and the fanny, but "Witold Gombrowicz" in subsequent novels spends less and less time explaining the events. His nonchalant conciseness reaches a peak in *Cosmos* where in the last two sentences of the novel he changes the subject very swiftly: after a description of a mountain episode during which Louis committed suicide, the narrator moves back to Warsaw and in the last sentence with apparent unconcern says: "Today we had chicken and rice for lunch." He is curt in describing Louis's suicide. Having discovered it, he returns to the picnicking friends without telling them about it and without being particularly agitated by it. "Mr. Witold" in *Pornografia* is likewise brief and calm in recording multiple murders committed at Powórna within a short span of time. The spare rhetoric of the narrator leaves to the reader the task of finding out what actually happened and why. It gives the reader substantial freedom of interpretation, and demands from him a much greater mental effort than do explicit nineteenth-century narratives. A rule may be posed that the less articulate the narrator, the greater the reader's freedom and difficulty of interpreting the text. For the same reason, then, Gombrowicz's novels grow progressively more difficult. In *Ferdydurke,* the narrator still talks a lot and wants to be the reader's guide. In *Pornografia* and *Cosmos,* he repeatedly leaves the reader in the dark.

Gombrowicz's narrators and stage producers represent different levels of maturity and intelligence, but they share similar desires and support each other in efforts to satisfy them. In particular, they share a sado-masochistic tendency. The plans of action conceived by the producers usually include a hurting of others: Frederick's plan to bring Karol and Henia together, and Gonzalez's suggestion that Ignac get rid of the dominance of his father by any method whatever, for example. The "rape" of Siphon and Leo's enjoyment of the embarrassment of others are further instances of sadistic pleasures. Gombrowicz's narrators cannot at first measure up to the producers in this respect. Johnnie in *Ferdydurke* is scandalized by the behavior of the boys at school. Soon, however, he loses the capacity to be so scandalized, and enjoys the havoc he has wrought in the house of the Youthfuls he then leaves to pursue a similar course in the country home he visits. "Mr. Gombrowicz" in *Trans-Atlantic* is easily led by Gonzalez; the two Witolds in *Pornografia* and *Cosmos* do not even need instruction in how to combine callousness and interest in watching others suffer, being as skilled at it as their mentors.

The masochistic tendency manifests itself in the persistence with which the narrators expose their own and the producers' secret desires and actions they both undertake to satisfy these. The dealings of the two friends scarcely ever evoke a reader's admiration. The storytellers know this, yet never cease to initiate the reader into every kind of unsavory design without the slightest concession to conventional morality or occasional introduction into their narration of a tone of genuine doubt or embarrassment, to soften the reader's assessment of them.

The sado-masochism of Gombrowicz's narrators has to do with the quality of his plots. There are in them many humdrum events that could happen in any life at any time; the beginnings of these novels present an ordinary world peopled with ordinary human beings. In each beginning, the place of action is usually an apartment room connoting the security and dullness of middle-class existence.[3] The narrators are "average" as is their power of observation and circle of acquaintances. However, owing to apparent sensitivity to, and enjoyment of, pain, their narration reveals a tendency toward bizarre interpretations of events and situations. They constantly perceive sinister omens in their surroundings, and await disasters both joyfully and fearfully. The safety pins in Katasia's room acquire symbolic meaning for Witold and Fuchs in *Cosmos;* Johnnie in *Ferdydurke* feels an irresistible desire to tear the wings and legs off a fly and throw it into Zuta's shoe. Later, he anticipates with fear and joy the fight between masters and servants in his aunt's home. "Mr. Gombrowicz" in *Trans-Atlantic* interprets the behavior of Gonzalez's servant as sadistic teasing. The expectations of the narrators are fulfilled: strange murders occur in God-fearing country homes and solid middle class citizens commit murders or kill themselves. The death or injury of human beings is often foreshadowed by torturings of animals. Someone hangs a sparrow next to the Wojtys' house, and Witold strangles Lena's favorite cat. The unexpected appearances of pain and the narrators' attitudes towards it destroy the surface realism of Gombrowicz's novels. At the outset, dull events occurring in the dull lives of middle class Polish citizens seem to be narrated. However, the instances of suffering narrated with teasing callousness by the speaker alert the reader to the fact that the speaker's way of presenting events may be biased and incomplete, requiring interpretation. The reader begins to look for symbolic meanings for the most trivial events.

François Bondy has observed that the motif of the duel often recurs in Gombrowicz's novels.[4] This motif may appear as a parody of the traditional duel where two adversaries fire at each other as happens with Major Kobrzycki and Gonzalez, and with Philifor and Anti-Philifor. It may be a duel of faces like the one fought by Mientus and Siphon, or be another form of competition, such as takes place between the young and the old in *Pornografia*. Bondy's observation can be extended to include all kinds of shifts in power that occur in Gombrowicz's novels.

The fundamental relation between individuals in Gombrowicz's novels involves domination and submission. It is never stable: the center of power may become the center of submission and vice versa. If at first A prevails over B, B tries to initiate actions eventually bringing about A's downfall. When this happens, A may or may not initiate actions which will in turn result in the downfall of B. This relationship is, in its simplest form embodied in the short stories where the same reversal always occurs: first A triumphs over B and then the opposite takes place. The novels contain several such reversals and several centers of power. The beginning of *Pornografia* presents an ordinary world in which customary relationships between adults dominating youngsters prevail. When Frederick and Witold arrive at Powórna, by virtue of their age they become members in an adult world which wields power over the world of Henia and Karol. Later, they surrender to a fascination with the teenagers, eventually working out a plan which returns them to a position of domination. They subjugate Henia and Karol, but do so in a way that is different from the "customary" one portrayed at the onset. While this is going on, other reversals occur. At first, Karol is under the spell of the underground officer Siemian, but at the end he loses all respect for him and even consents to murder him. He now wields power over Siemian instead of standing ready to take Siemian's orders. Another reversal is the surrender of power by Lady Amelia. Once an indisputable leader of her circle of acquaintances, Amelia becomes so fascinated by Frederick that she loses her attitude of power in regard to such obvious inferiors as the farmboy caught by her in the pantry. Likewise, *Trans-Atlantic* is a kaleidoscope of reversals which occur between the narrator and Gonzalez; between these two and Major Kobrzycki; be-

tween Ignac and his father; between the narrator and the Order
of the Spur and so on.

Characteristically, the most important of these duels of wills,
or shifts of power, do not lead to the establishment of a stable
final situation but always to some form of chaos in which the
duelers lose their faces or their Form. In other words, there
are no permanent victories in Gombrowicz's world. Everything
ends in a draw. This draw, called "the wriggling heap" in
Ferdydurke, expresses one of the most important novelistic
intuitions of Gombrowicz. While the pugnacious nature of his
characters reflects their sado-masochistic tendency (both winning and losing affords them an enjoyment), the outcome of
their duels suggests that they have learned something from
having exercised their impulses and desires. They have acquired
a certain degree of understanding that a "moderate climate"
rather than "excessive ranges of temperature" is their natural
milieu; and that the semblance of maturity and wisdom which
they have so carefully cultivated is not worth maintaining. At
the conclusions of the duels, the motif of sado-masochism fades,
with the idea of man's perpetual immaturity gaining in importance. The narrator of *Ferdydurke* explicitly speaks of his new
understanding of human beings. The narrators in other novels
are less explicit, but convey the same idea by concluding the
novel with, or evoking in an important section of the novel, the
image of "the wriggling heap."

In other words, the sado-masochistic motif prominent in
Gombrowicz's novels influences both the plot and its narration.
This motif's importance, however, is secondary to that of such
motifs as the ambiguous relation between maturity and immaturity, the desire to assert oneself and the ability to develop.
Sado-masochism is a bait with which author Gombrowicz teases
the reader in the hope that attracted by it, the reader will swal-
low the author's perception of the world.

Sex is also a prominent motif in Gombrowicz's novels. It is
never introduced by means of the conventional love story:
boys do not meet girls, for example. Sex in Gombrowicz appears as homosexuality (*Pornografia, Ferdydurke, Cosmos, Trans-
Atlantic*), voyeurism (*Pornografia, Cosmos*), masturbation (*Cosmos*), pimping (*Pornografia*). The obstinacy with which Gom-

browicz's narrators return to the metonyms of touching and tasting reveal their oral and anal fixations. Given these situations, nobody lives happily ever after as a result of sexual attraction—or for that matter wants to. Most sexual encounters have to do with the narrator and the stage producer. These two, unable to develop and sustain warm human relationships, seek encounters which will afford them the amount of confusion and misfortune they crave for themselves—and for others. They do not want the "happy ever after" ending. *Ferdydurke* ends in an ironic account of a traditional love story in which the narrator unwillingly participates though it nauseates and annoys him. The lack of conventional sexual encounters has also to do with Gombrowicz's portrayal of women who, as will be argued in chapter eight, are schematized completely out of existence in his novels.

An interesting structural tendency arises as a result of Gombrowicz's concern for demonstrating man's capacity for development. The major characters (the narrators in particular) are led in the course of the novel from a closed to an open space, or from a place of striving and confinement to one of relaxation and freedom.[5] The action of *Ferdydurke* begins in a closed room and ends in a country field. The initial place of action in *Trans-Atlantic* is the room in which the narrator writes his story; the final place is the Argentinian countryside. *Cosmos* begins with the drudgery of finding a room in which to live (soon found), and ends on a mountain scene. The return to Warsaw mentioned in the last sentence is the only variation on the pattern. *Pornografia* opens with an account of a discussion conducted in a small room in a Warsaw apartment, and ends with a meeting of the four accomplices to murder. Meeting outside the room in which the crime was committed, they experience a moment of relaxation: "And for a split second, all four of us smiled."

The change in novelistic space is accompanied by a change in the character's life situation. The small room in which the narrator finds himself at the beginning goes together with his feeling of discomfort at being imposed upon by others (*Ferdydurke*), discomfort and vague dissatisfaction with life (*Cosmos*), pessimism (*Trans-Atlantic*), and anxiety (*Pornografia*). At the end, the narrators achieve a measure of freedom from anxiety and dominance by others. The final situation may include disappointment (*Ferdydurke, Cosmos*), but usually an increased sense of freedom also. The process of leaving the room or place of "confinement and striving" is usually described in great detail. Examples are Mientus' and Johnnie's trip to the country through the suburbs of Warsaw, the ride on horseback from Buenos Aires to Gonzalez's hacienda, and the trip to the mountains in *Cosmos*.

II   Ferdydurke: *The Emergence of "Form"*

To many people, Gombrowicz is still the author of *Ferdydurke* "and some other works." *Ferdydurke* became very popular in Poland after World War II and was the first book of Gombrowicz to be translated into other languages: French (1958); German (1960); English and Italian (1961); Dutch (1962); Spanish (1964); Danish (1967); Swedish and Norwegian (1969). Yet to see Gombrowicz as the author of this novel only is like considering Dostoevsky as primarily the author of *Notes from the Underground*. The essential concerns of both writers are present in these works. Both authors, however, dramatized these concerns much more fully in subsequent works.

From the vantage point of the later works *Ferdydurke* is by no means the best of Gombrowicz's novels. It has aged; some of the metonyms on which it so heavily relies (the thighs of the modern girl, the countenances of Mr. and Mrs. Youthful, the master-servant rivalry) have lost much of their pungency. However, what remains is substantial enough to establish *Ferdydurke* as a key to Gombrowicz's works. For the first time the relation between perpetually immature individuals receives the writer's undivided attention.

As opposed to the other three novels, *Ferdydurke* is not a continuous narrative but a sequence of three important episodes in the life of the narrator and two philosophical tales tucked in between these episodes. The tales have no direct connection with the plot, and occasionally, they have been detached from the work in which they originally appeared: in 1957, they were published in the collection of short stories *Bakakaj*.

Ferdydurke was first published in 1937 by Rój, the same publishing house which brought out the *Memoir from Adolescence*. A second Polish edition appeared in 1957, containing certain changes. The classroom scenes in part one were shortened and the "Introduction to Philimor Honeycombed with Childishness" was reworked so that ascerbic passages such as the one about the relationship between writers and readers disappeared. This revised version has been included in the *Collected Works* and is the basis for the English translation.

Tadeusz Kępiński writes in his book on Gombrowicz about the models for the characters in *Ferdydurke,* Johnnie, Professor Pimko, Mientus and Siphon, Zuta, Philifor and Philimor.[6] He believes that Pimko and other professors in the book were modelled on the professors of the Wielopolski Gymnasium which he and Gombrowicz attended. Mientus and Siphon were modelled on two Wielopolski students. One of them, nicknamed Mr. Chairman, was always eager to follow the rules; the other, a cynical and clever fellow, eventually dropped out of school. Zuta was a caricature of a certain Anielka, the sister of one of Gombrowicz's schoolmates. The names of the characters in the two philosophical tales were derived from *Analyse du Jeu des Echecks* by the eighteenth-century French chess player Philidor. Gombrowicz's early interest in philosophy (he read Kant at the age of sixteen) accounts for the topic of the first tale. Finally, Johnnie was an ironic portrait of Gombrowicz himself.

Kępiński's account invites further speculations about the origin of the title word and the particularly sarcastic presentation of Pimko. The word *Ferdydurke* (which does not appear in the text and which did not exist in the Polish language until the popularity of the novel introduced it there) is an alias of little Johnnie, as Gombrowicz confirms in his *Journal* (VI, 174). It carries the echoes of Dostoevsky's Ferdyshchenko who, like Johnnie, had difficulties in maintaining his adult independence. Obviously, Gombrowicz did not fully sympathize with his downtrodden hero.

As to Pimko, the professor from Cracow, none of the professors at Wielopolski Gymnasium bore a name even remotely resembling this one. "Pimko" suggests the name of the well known Mickiewicz scholar Stanisław Pigoń, a professor at the

Jagiellonian University in Cracow during Gombrowicz's adolescence, whose work was almost exclusively devoted to the
Polish romantic tradition. Pigoń's style has been caricatured in
Pimko's way of speaking and in the classroom scene during
which the name of Słowacki is invoked. This style abounded in
laudatory adjectives and lofty phrases glorifying the romantic
bards. In 1934, Pigoń published his key work: *Pan Tadeusz:
Wzrost, Wielkość, Sława* (*Pan Tadeusz: Its Growth, Reputation,
and Greatness*). In 1929 he edited the *Complete Works* of Adam
Mickiewicz.

The plot of *Ferdydurke* centers around little Johnnie, an
involuntary pupil and protégé of the renowned pedagogue Professor Pimko. Johnnie is in fact a thirty-year old writer who has
been patronized and patted on the head by the "cultural aunts
and uncles" until he lost his resistance and allowed others to
overwhelm him with their *Besserwissenschaft*. Johnnie then
goes back to school where he meets boys like himself, frustrated
individuals who ineffectively rebel against their counselors and
supervisors.

In part two Johnnie is placed as a boarder in the home of
Mr. and Mrs. Youthful, a progressive Warsaw couple whose
daughter Zuta is a perfect modern coed. He soon discovers that
the self-assurance of the Youthfuls and their unshaken belief
in progress are rooted in an adoration of their daughter whose
aloofness fascinates and flatters them. By upsetting Zuta's self-
sufficiency Johnnie destroys the smugness of the Youthfuls, their
social optimism and conviction that given a chance, people will
behave the way progressive social theories say they should
behave. Johnnie leaves the Youthfuls with the feeling of well-
executed revenge and with an emerging conviction that maturity
is inevitably a sham.

In part three he goes to the country where he hopes to find
authenticity. He is accompanied by his schoolmate Mientus on
whose initiative the trip has been undertaken. It turns out,
however, that people in the country are just as conditioned by
others as those in the city, and that authenticity is nowhere
to be found. Instead of rivalry between pupils and teachers,
or adults and youngsters, there exists here a similar rivalry
between masters and servants. The farmboy whom Mientus

so hopes to find turns out to be different from what the city-educated, middle class boy imagined him to be. Johnnie in any case succeeds in upsetting the order of the country just as he upset it in the city. He and Mientus escape, leaving a "wriggling heap" behind.

The two tales "Philifor Honeycombed with Childishness" and "Philimor Honeycombed with Childishness" resemble *Candide* and *Rasselas* in their style and directness of message. They both illustrate the principle that men are not masters of the Form which they create, but on the contrary, are its slaves. Man's behavior and convictions do not grow from his "essential self" but arise according to a logic independent of its subjects. In Gombrowicz's words, when people say A, they feel obliged to say B and C without being sure why they do so, much less why they said A in the first place. Their behavior and words *create them* and not the other way around. All human beings are like the lady who said: "How can I know what I think until I hear what I say?" In the Philifor tale Professors Philifor and Anti-Philifor represent, respectively, higher analysis and higher synthesis. Therefore, they feel obliged to be at war with each other. Their minds having been formed by some omnipresent pedagogy, they cannot move beyond a set of principles instilled in them at some indeterminable moment in their past. When the professors meet eye to eye, a duel follows, which produces some truly unforeseeable situations. The self-confidence of the professors breaks down. For, like most people, they lose the air of self-importance upon meeting the unexpected. They turn out to be "unfinished" and uncertain of their principles. Each of them having "existed" largely through the support received from his adversary now loses his basis of existential support. Their new attitude is expressed by Philifor in the final phrase of the tale addressed to the narrator: "My child, everything is honeycombed with childishness."

The Philimor tale shows the absurd chain of events generated by a mishap at a tennis tournament. The story about the descendant of an eighteenth-century French peasant begins at a tournament in which the great-great-grandson of the peasant participates. The match is interrupted by someone shooting at the ball and ends with one of the ladies having a miscarriage.

In between, Form reigns: people react in accordance with what they feel to be proper behavior at any given moment. Nothing is done for its own sake; actions are motivated by others rather than by the actors themselves.

III *Parody in* Ferdydurke

Ferdydurke is a multilevel parody in which three things are consecutively parodied in the three sections of the book: traditional schooling and some of the authors who influenced Gombrowicz but with whom he disagreed; a new generation, the likes of Monsieur Homais; and self-conscious refinement and cultivation in general. The parodic effects owe much to the tone of voice of the narrator, sly and sarcastic in his descriptions of people and events which give him little pleasure since he is often their victim. The enjoyment of the parodies, however, is shared by the author and the reader. *Ferdydurke* is one of the most amusing serious novels in Polish literature. Here is a sample of the school lore from part one:

The master: 'Well, then, why does Słowacki arouse our admiration, love, and esctasy? . . . Because, gentlemen, Słowacki was a great poet. Walkiewicz, tell me why! Tell me, Walkiewicz.'
. . . .
'Because he was a great poet, sir,' said Walkiewicz.
. . . .
Kotecki: Heaven help me, sir, but how am I to be sent into transports of delight, if I am not sent into transports of delight?
. . . .
The master: 'For heaven's sake hold your tongue, Kotecki. You are trying to ruin me. No marks for Kotecki. He does not realize what he is saying.'
Kotecki: 'You have explained this, sir, but I am not sent into transports of delight.'
. . . .
The master: 'Kotecki, I have a wife and a young child. At least have pity on the child, Kotecki. . . .'[7]

The satire here is directed against the type of schooling which relies heavily on memorization and the teacher's authority, as well as against propagating cults of the romantic bards at schools of the type described here.

The most prominent of literary parodies is that of "the boys' theme" in *The Brothers Karamazov*. Siphon is a caricature of Alesha while the schoolboys are caricatures of those boys in *The Brothers Karamazov* who so quickly changed from nasty brats to little angels.[8] The narrator is unaware of this parody which becomes the sole property of author and reader.

Behind these humorous treatments there lies another level of parody, more complicated and less richly entertaining. It was first noticed by the Polish critic Arthur Sandauer who observed that didactic pedagogy, the cult of progress and the belief in crystal palaces satirized in *Ferdydurke* are among the "ingredients" of modern Polish culture[9] which has tended to accept the value of traditional schooling and the belief that education ("dished out" to the masses according to a prescription of some pundits) will automatically bring progress and general welfare. It has tended to emphasize the reading of poetry over the material aspects of existence. Sandauer deals in intuitions rather than statistical facts, and for that reason can be easily attacked by someone whose intuitions happen to be different. He is, however, a serious critic whose insights have often withstood the test of time. His suggestion about Gombrowicz's critical attitude toward many aspects of Polish culture seems correct. This level of parody is, of course, also beyond the reach of the narrator. It arises from events of the story rather than from the commentary and tone of little Johnnie.

The Polish novelist and critic Bruno Schulz spoke of yet another level of parodic meaning in *Ferdydurke*.[10] In his view, *Ferdydurke* reveals the existence of a secret world within each person, a world which is a distorted version of officially accepted values and ideas. Less like the world of the Freudian or Jungian subconscious than a "basement of culture" and its vulgar and unsavory version, it consists of "inferior myths, second class beauties, shoddy charms and dubious graces." This subculture has its own secret submythology which is a parody of the official mythology. People pretend that they do not share it with one another. They express views that are mature, cultivated and in agreement with the spirit of the times. In the sewers of

their minds, however, they collect "the refuse of civilization,"
judgments and opinions which often run counter to what they
profess aloud. This submythology is grounded in immature
desires and inadmissible priorities. Its secret hierarchy dominates
men more than they are willing to admit.

The parody described by Schulz is not Gombrowicz's creation.
It is a phenomenon of life. Gombrowicz merely verbalized its
existence for the reader. Or, more accurately, Gombrowicz's
narrator did. He spoke extensively about the shoddy and immature desires which he discovers in such "mature" characters as
Pimko and the country squires. The narrator, the author, and
the reader come to the same realization of the phenomenon of
human immaturity. The parody of official values we perceive in
the characters of the story affords scant entertainment, but provides us with a feeling that we understand life.

IV   Language and "Form"

An inventive work from the point of view of language,
Ferdydurke contains a number of expressions which have
become part of the Polish language. Some are neologisms,
others are metaphorical or specialized uses of already existing
words. They include Form (*Forma*), a child's fanny or backside (*pupa*), fitting someone with a fanny or a backside (*upupienie*), mug (*gęba*), and fitting someone with a mug (*przyprawienie gęby*). These expressions have entered the Polish
language in much the same way new meaning of the surname
"Prufrock" became a part of the English language after T. S.
Eliot's poem gained notoriety.

"To fit someone with a fanny" means to coerce someone to
behave in an apprehensive, insecure way, to make him feel
small and immature. Behavioral psychology describes this
situation as forcing someone to be the child, while we ourselves may play the role of parent. People who have been so
coerced have "fannies" i.e., others created their personalities for
them. "To fit someone with a mug" describes a similar situation,
but the emphasis here is not so much condescension as the forcing of some kind of pose, or face, on someone. "The mug" is
the face and body expression we assume upon confronting others.

Like the fanny, it is a "creation" of another person, and not what we would like to think of as our own innermost self. People fitted with a mug or a fanny have been shaped by others to the point that they behave like actors on a stage. They do not play themselves but some other person; they carry the attitude of examinee into their adulthood; they live borrowed lives.

The heroes of *Ferdydurke* are divided into those who fit others with fannies and mugs—and their victims. The positions of victims and persecutors are not stable: Johnnie is fitted with a mug and a fanny by Pimko and the Youthfuls, but he reciprocates generously at the conclusion. Hierarchies exist among the fitters and the "fittees." A may patronize B and thus fit him with a fanny, but A may himself be in an inferior position in regard to C.

Gombrowicz's use of the word Form is more difficult to explain. He used it throughout his writing career, from *Ferdydurke* to his late essays and interviews. Always capitalized, Form was one of his favorite terms. *Ferdydurke* presents Form as the totality of communicative efforts between people, all that arises as a result of the duel of wills and efforts to fit others with fannies and mugs. In *A Kind of Testament*, however, Gombrowicz underlines that to reduce his view on Form to the mere idea that men shape each other is a simplification:

To start with, let us say that the deformation produced between men is not the only deformation, if only because man, in his deepest essence, possesses something which I would call "the Formal Imperative." Something which is, it seems to me, indispensable to any organic creation. For instance, take our innate need to complete incomplete Form: every Form that has been started requires a complement. When I say A, something compels me to say B, and so on. This need to develop, to complete, because of a certain logic inherent in Form, plays an important part in my work.[11]

Form, then, contains a modification of the concept of *homo faber*: what is produced are not material artifacts but a web of relationships, an elusive "placing in the context," an economy of effort and result. Man can be described only in terms of Form: the rest cannot be "formalized" and therefore is beyond the reach of discussion.

Form is necessary and inevitable; it is also undesirable. Form is our natural element; it also disfigures us. This seems to be a contradition of Gombrowicz's art, and one, Czesław Miłosz wrote, that Gombrowicz never resolved.[12] It is possible, however, to view Form as a complex process which ranges from self-affirmation to self-destruction. "The formal imperative" of which Gombrowicz speaks, the desire for Form, is very closely connected with life itself. To live means to produce Form, an activity which ceases only with death. In this sense, there is no escape from Form. The "spinning of Form," however, can overwhelm the spinner as well as the others; an illusion may arise, for example, that Form is identical with man rather than a product of man's activity.

Gombrowicz once said that the secret of *Ferdydurke* lies in the perfect symmetry between the tales of Philifor and Philimor. The symmetry seems to consist in both tales following the principle of causality as opposed to the principle of purposiveness. "Gombrowicz . . . does not play with a lack of causality, as many contemporary writers do . . . but with a lack of purpose," remarked Sandauer.[13] Indeed, both tales are series of automatic actions which are interpreted by onlookers and participants as purposeful actions. In the Philimor tale the shipowner's wife witnesses her husband being shot in the neck. She wants to revenge herself on the wrongdoer, but unable to reach him, she slaps her neighbor's face instead. The man who was slapped, an epileptic, has an attack as a result of the slapping. In the Philifor tale, the wife of the Master of higher synthesis was hit by the Master of higher analysis. The Master of higher synthesis hits the mistress of the Master of higher analysis in return. Both adversaries seem to behave with some aim in view, when, in fact, they have no such aim. They only react to each other. In a less obvious way, the same happens in the other parts of *Ferdydurke*. The ideological declarations of Pimko, the Youthfuls, Mientus, and Siphon are but surface phenomena. What actually happens is that the characters are tossed in various directions by "waves" made by other people. Johnnie remarks in part three that the masters eat to spite the servants and the servants behave stupidly to spite the masters. The duels of wills are in large measure reactions to others rather than purposeful actions.

Gombrowicz's perception of human beings in *Ferdydurke* is diametrically opposed to perceptions of many novelists who were his contemporaries. His characters, deprived of substance, are like the points which come to being as a result of the crossing of lines of Form. We are, *Ferdydurke* tells us, always and everywhere unfinished creatures, neither-nors. Our life position, the country of our birth, family and wealth, all are props which help support our fictitious wholeness. When the rhythm of life is destroyed and when instead of our place in the social grid we are forced by circumstances into "the wriggling heap," our Form falls off for a while allowing our essential formlessness to show. Human beings are not solitary *Steppenwolves* who always preserve their essential selves intact no matter what the circumstances are. They are not creatures following the secret logic of the subconscious. Gombrowicz has little use for the regularities implied by depth psychology or the neo-romantic vision of man found in Herman Hesse. His characters are created by one another in a random way. At the end of *Ferdydurke* Johnnie comes to the realization that there is no escape from the process of being created by others. He may thus, appropriately be called the first structuralist hero, one consciously consenting to being shaped by others and willingly shaping others in return.

V   Trans-Atlantic: *The Art of Unlearning*

The title in Polish is *Trans-Atlantyk,* a new usage. It brings to mind the adjective *transatlantycki,* transatlantic, yet the author wished the title to mean *Across the Atlantic:* a look at Poland from across the Atlantic.[14] This is the most Poland-oriented of Gombrowicz's books—in the same sense in which Faulkner's novels have the South as their central hero. Paradoxically, this is also the only novel of Gombrowicz which narrates events that do not take place in Poland. Its place of action is Argentina.

Trans-Atlantic, written with a sense of humor which ranges from benevolent to gently satirical, is a delightful Rabelaisian account of Gombrowicz's first years in Argentina. It is also a serious study of the change of heart concerning his heritage which the narrator undergoes under the influence of a foreign milieu.

Trans-Atlantic has been called a novel for convenience's sake; in fact, it is written in the style of the old Polish *gawęda*, a literary genre which imitates spoken, rather than written, narrative. The narrator in *Trans-Atlantic* tells the story in a manner similar to that used by *raconteurs,* as opposed to writers. His sentences are spoken sentences, full of exclamatory words, unfinished phrases and the spelling which follows pronunciation instead of orthography. The speaker practices what Northrop Frye calls associative speaking—the slightly incoherent way of stringing sentences together in a casual conversation. This kind of narration brings forth the elements of intonation and natural turns of phrase which often disappear from written texts. The speaker in *Trans-Atlantic* is an actor as well as a narrator: his rhythms of speech and abundant colloquialisms require reading aloud. *Trans-Atlantic* is one of those prose narratives which should be performed rather than read.

The genre of *gawęda* which the work follows goes back to such sixteenth and seventeenth century works as Mikołaj Rej's *The Good Man's Life* (*Żywot człowieka poczciwego*) and Jan Chryzostom Pasek's *Memoirs* (*Pamiętniki*). These two works were not conceived as works of fiction: Pasek's is a private memoir which charms and amuses the contemporary reader by the good stories it tells and the narrative tone which is boastful, naïve and sly at the same time. Rej's work describes how a man should live in order to be satisfied with life. It combines didacticism and good practical sense. The best known *gawęda* is Henryk Rzewuski's *Memoirs of Seweryn Soplica, Esq.* (*Pamiątki Imć Pana Seweryna Soplicy*, 1839), a fictionalized account of the colorful life of the eighteenth century Polish nobility. The *gawęda* has much in common with the Russian *skaz*, a narrative which likewise imitates spoken language. The narrator in the *skaz*, however, is usually an uneducated peasant. The charm and humor of such classical *skaz* narratives as Nikolai Leskov's *The Steel Flea* (1881) derive from the distance in social levels between the narrator and his readers: the narrator is simpleminded and humble, a fact which the readers are meant to perceive. The *gawęda* narrator is conceited and boastful, often using Latin and stressing his high station in life. His perceptions are those of an educated person. The *gawęda* narrator is funny because of his boastfulness, but the *skaz* narrator's humility makes him funny too. Both types of narration are polyphonic owing to the personalties of the narrators, since reader and the narrator are likely to differ in their interpretations of events. This is also true of certain kinds of satire such as Swift's *A Modest Proposal;* the *skaz* and the *gawęda,* however, are good-natured rather than bitter in tone, and meant to delight rather than rouse indignation. In the American tradition, the Uncle Remus stories can be compared to the *skaz;* the tall tales of the frontier such as those attributed to Davy Crockett bear some similarity to the *gawęda.*

Gombrowicz never uses any existing genre without parodying it, and *Trans-Atlantic* is no exception. The parody of the *gawęda* is brought about through the tone of the narrator. Instead of being naïvely boastful all the time, the narrator often assumes a tone of sly humility, and even speaks of himself in a deprecatory manner. Not that he spares others, but he disapproves of himself as well and does it awkwardly and naïvely, thus making the reader laugh. This combination of self-deprecation and humor reminds one of the narrator in Rabelais's *Gargantua and Pantagruel* who likewise strove to evoke laughter at the expense of the characters of whom he spoke, as well as at his own expense.

The genre of the *gawęda* has seldom been used in recent Polish literature. Generally Polish novelists have been following western European trends rather than the resources of Poland's literary past. Gombrowicz's use of this archaic genre reflects his desire to turn Polish readers' attention away from largely derivative nineteenth-century literature toward the worthwhile and neglected parts of Polish cultural heritage dating back to the Renaissance and the baroque period.

The linguistic experiments of *Trans-Atlantic* have a similar purpose. They bring forth similarities between baroque Polish and contemporary peasant dialects, thus suggesting that peasants have kept alive at least a small portion of the baroque heritage whereas the educated class abandoned it altogether.

Trans-Atlantic is the most inventive work of Gombrowicz

from the point of view of language. The narrator mixes archaic Polish and contemporary peasant dialects, capitalizes words in the middle of a sentence creating unusual intonations, and uses archaic and peasant phraseology to describe situations and events calling for standard Polish. The dialects of Polish have preserved many features of seventeenth-century speech, e.g., a single conjugation for the first person plural in present tense (seventeenth-century Polish has *zapalemy, wstydziemy, prowadziemy* and so do contemporary dialects).[15] Thus in many cases Gombrowicz's archaisms sound like the speech of uneducated people and vice versa: his renditions of peasant speech bring to mind seventeenth-century literary Polish. This vacillation of meaning differs greatly from such attempts to use dialect to convey local color as those of Stanisław Reymont and Kazimierz Tetmajer: Reymont's to enhance the realism of his novels about peasants, and Tetmajer's to convey the atmosphere of the Carpathian mountains. Such uses of dialect are easy to translate. One need only substitute some narrowly local pronunciation or spelling for the dialect words. When the dialect carries the double burden of removing the quality of gentility from the narrative and of archaizing, the translator is faced with unsurmountable difficulties. It is not surprising that as of this writing, there has been no translation of *Trans-Atlantic* into English.

In *A Kind of Testament* Gombrowicz summarizes the book thus:

In an archaic prose, as though it were set in the distant past, I tell how, just before the war, I landed in the Argentine, how war broke out when I was there. I, Gombrowicz, make the acquaintance of a *puto* (a queer) who is in love with a young Pole, and circumstances make me arbiter of the situation: I can throw the young man into the queer's arms or make him stay with his father, a very honourable, dignified and old-fashioned Polish major.
To throw him into the *puto*'s arms is to deliver him up to vice, to set him on roads which lead nowhere, into the troubled waters of the abnormal, perhaps, of limitless liberty, of an uncontrollable future. To wrench him away from the queer and make him return to his father is to keep him within the confines of the honest Polish

tradition. What should I choose? Fidelity to the past ... or the freedom to create oneself as one will?[16]

This conflict comes to a climax when Major Kobrzycki becomes aware of the goings-on and decides to kill his son rather than give him up to vice. At the same time, the *puto* Gonzalez tries to persuade Kobrzycki's son Ignac to do away with his father and start living for himself. He also tries to convince the narrator (named Witold Gombrowicz) that this is the right way to go. The narrator is bound by oath to the secret organization called The Order of the Silver Spur whose members torment one another and daydream about glorious and awe-inspiring feats which they will some day perform to save Poland. They finally decide to murder Ignac and by the cruelty and senselessness of this murder frighten the enemy. These plans of mutual extermination reach an unexpected conclusion on the last pages of the novel.

Trans-Atlantic conveys the state of mind of a Pole facing both East and West. This attitude has much in common with the attitude of any minority person (national, racial, or psychological) confronted by his or her minority culture and the prevailing culture of the time. In such a situation different people behave differently, and Gombrowicz demonstrates many such behavior patterns in the book.

He starts his settling of accounts with his heritage by satirizing it. In the first part of the book, the Polish characters are shown in their most stereotyped poses and actions. The narrator describes a number of people who can be said to play the game of "we also can" and "we also have that." The Polish ambassador to Argentina tries very hard to show his hosts that Poland has produced many great men and that the courage and bravery of her citizens are remarkable. Members of the Polish community in Buenos Aires flatter one another by mouthing patriotic slogans and recollecting the past glories of the nation. They are extremely sensitive to being slighted at cocktail parties they attend; whenever feeling they do not receive proper attention, they begin to play the "we also have that" game with increased energy.

The characters continue to respect old class divisions while engaging in ego games with the outside world. The aristocratic baron looks down upon his partners in business, Ciumkała and Pyzdral (both of these are peasant names), who in turn resent the baron and purposely embarrass him by their coarse behavior. They do so individually, however, rather than through any feeling of solidarity for one another. The irony of the situation is that no one here can live without the other: the skills of the refugees are closely interconnected. Instead of recognizing this and seeking a *modus vivendi* transcending differences of background and habit, they try to put down their partners at every opportunity. A similarly absurd situation takes place in the mysterious basement where the Knights of the Order of the Spur secretly gather. Their only occupation is the thrusting of spurs into one another's legs and watching the expression of pain on the face of the victim. They imagine that by so doing they "keep the faith" and further the national cause. Their high-sounding phrases echo the language of Henryk Sienkiewicz's *Trilogy* (1884-88) as well as Professor Pimko's lectures to little Johnnie.

The narrator is only partially aware of all these ruses. He records the behavior of people without fully understanding it. The reader is expected to see farther and deeper than the narrator and share with the author an enjoyment of the situational ironies. The narrator, however, is observant enough to understand that there is something profoundly wrong with the attitude of the characters he describes, and that it is probably a good idea to break away from the ways and habits of his minority group. His first step is to refuse to return to Europe with the same passengers with whom he arrived. He remains in Argentina and tries to start a new life instead. His second step involves becoming responsive to suggestions and arguments of Gonzalez, who becomes a guide in the narrator's exploration of the psychology of his minority group. Why, asks Gonzalez in his conversations with the narrator, should one always honor the father before even considering the son? Why should the safe ways of fatherland be always preferred to the uncertain explorations of the sonland? What makes it inadvisable to take risks in self-development?

Gonzalez's questioning applies first of all to the citizens of eastern Europe who have been asked to do much more for their fatherlands during the last two centuries than the citizens of western Europe during the same period. It also applies to those who hesitate between personal development and loyalty to their own national, racial or minority group. In short, behind the political question lies the psychological one. As Gombrowicz states it elsewhere, is the attitude of the hobo preferable to that of the miser? The miser chooses the safe way; he piles up his treasures in a secret place and forgets about the world in contemplating them. The hobo recklessly sets out on a journey whose destination is uncertain. The Knights of the Order of the Spur are the misers who sit in the cellar contemplating values they profess. Gonzalez encourages the narrator to be a hobo and press forward at any price. The miser's fate is predictable: he will wither away with his riches. The hobo's fate is unsure: he may perish even more miserably than the miser, or he may find in his travels riches that will surpass those of the miser. Misers usually try to induce everyone to live the way they do— and so do hobos. Gonzalez suggests that a minority person has no choice but to elect one or the other of these attitudes. Either be the hobo or the miser, either the father or the son. There is no third choice.

Does the narrator follow this suggestion? The plot of *Trans-Atlantic* ends inconclusively, with an outburst of laughter in which all adversaries participate. Matters are not brought to a point where what route the narrator has chosen becomes clear. The plot also turns out to be a poor guide in this respect. The narrator sympathizes with both parties, and is only too glad to declare a truce between the warring sides. At the end, we witness a moment of tolerance instead of a "night of the long knives." This seems not to be the answer to Gonzalez's impassioned pleas, however. Indeed, a look at the structure of the book shows that author Gombrowicz has more to say on the subject than narrator Gombrowicz.

VI *Literary Parodies in* Trans-Atlantic

Trans-Atlantic has parodic structure. Its verbal acrobatics and mockery of the most stereotyped Polish attitudes are but

the surface of a more ambitious aim—to parody Adam Mickiewicz's *Pan Tadeusz* (1834) and Henryk Sienkiewicz's *Trilogy*
(1888). The parody is accomplished by a recasting of these
latter two works in baroque phraseology and mode of being.

When he began writing *Trans-Atlantic,* a conviction began
to ripen in Gombrowicz that original and vital elements of
Polish culture were rooted in the baroque period rather than
in the romantic or post-romantic one. He began to believe
that an undercurrent of Polish culture ran through baroque
exuberance, detectable in a lack of inhibitions and enjoyment
of life's unsophisticated pleasures. The melancholy patriotic
pathos of the romantics is an element alien to it. While most
Polish thinkers and artists paid this element homage, it remains,
he felt, an artificial ingredient in the Polish way of being. Con-
sequently, Gombrowicz's ambition was to bring this state of
affairs out into the open and to challenge Polish cultural consciousness by doing so. He wanted to reawaken the baroque
sensibility and do away with what he perceived to be romantic
fallacy. In order to accomplish this, he bypassed the nineteenth
century altogether, returning to the seventeenth century for
his models of language and the narrator's way of looking at
events. His *Trans-Atlantic* is wordy like the seventeenth- and
eighteenth-century Polish narratives. It relies heavily on the
device of metonymy as opposed to romantic metaphor. Its characters think and behave in a way which makes them akin to
the world of Pasek rather than that of Mickiewicz or Sienkiewicz.

In many ways, *Trans-Atlantic* is an ironic response to Sienkiewicz's *Trilogy.* Both Gombrowicz and Sienkiewicz used Pasek
as a source. Sienkiewicz, however, endowed his heroes with a
romantic sensibility while Gombrowicz tried to preserve the
spirit as well as the letter of Pasek's writing.[17] The characters
created by the three writers speak a similar language. The meaning of words in Sienkiewicz, however, is influenced by the
romantic tradition. His narrator is a man full of nineteenth-
century neuroses and inhibitions. Gombrowicz's narrator does
not censor or edit his thoughts as he passes them along to the
reader, but conveys immediate observations about the physical
details of the world he sees, touches, and smells. Sienkiewicz's
narrator offers generalizations based on these physical observa-

tions. He tells us what his characters look like in general rather than what they appear to be at a given moment. Sienkiewicz's narrator is deadly serious about the events and feelings he describes. He is unable to look at them from a distance or acknowledge the possibility of a point of view different from his own. Gombrowicz's narrator is laxer in this respect, well able to laugh at himself and the point of view he represents. He would like to persuade his readers that this point of view is correct, but does not preach it or pretend that his is the only and absolute truth. Also, Sienkiewicz and Gombrowicz differ in their use of seventeenth-century phraseology. In Sienkiewicz, the characters use archaisms, but the narrator tends to follow contemporary standard Polish. In Gombrowicz, the opposite takes place. The narrator's language is archaic and slangy at the same time while the characters use the phraseology particular to the twentieth-century social strata they represent. Finally, Sienkiewicz's narrator is a virtuous man while Gombrowicz's is not. At the same time, he is closer to life and more genuine than Sienkiewicz's, open to experience but not deprived of convictions. His imperfections give him a credibility which Sienkiewicz's narrator is likely to lack in the eyes of a contemporary reader. Gombrowicz's narrator emerges victorious from his duel with a nineteenth-century predecessor.

Adam Mickiewicz's *Pan Tadeusz* has also played an integral part in Polish cultural tradition. Written in exile, it describes the country of the exile's childhood. It ends with a nostalgic dream of the countryside which does not change with the times but forever preserves the atmosphere of an eighteenth-century village. From the standpoint of *Trans-Atlantic*, Mickiewicz's central thought of returning to lost innocence appears to be a variation on the return to the womb motif, a weakness of heart and mind rather than endorsement of virtue. Gombrowicz's characters live far away from Poland, but none of them daydreams about the beauties of lost childhood. They do not really think about going back to Poland (as does Mickiewicz's poetic speaker), partly because this is technically impossible (Major Kobrzycki) and partly because they often choose not to do so (the narrator and the Polish community in Argentina). It should be added that in eastern Europe emigration has generally been

socially disapproved of by the intelligentsia unless its reasons
are political. A Pole or Russian who leaves his country and
stays abroad for reasons similar to those of the narrator in *Trans-
Atlantic* is viewed with suspicion by his compatriots. Mickiewicz's narrator belongs with the majority: it is obvious to him
that given a chance, every Pole will return to "the country of
his childhood." Mickiewicz addresses his epic to the virtuous
Polish peasant who, of course, has never traveled abroad and
who might read *Pan Tadeusz* at some future time. Gombrowicz's
narrator understands very well that a Pole may choose to live
abroad, as he himself does. More realistically he addresses his
"family and friends" rather than the nation at large. The story
he tells is compared to "the stale noodles and rotten turnips
seasoned with the grease of sin." In Mickiewicz's narrative, the
exile walks on the noisy streets of a foreign city thinking about
his only consolation: the evening chat with his fellow exiles.
The exile's feelings and virtue remain unaffected by the new
conditions of life. *Trans-Atlantic* concentrates on a change of
heart, and the story it narrates is well seasoned with "the
grease of sin."

There are many striking similarities between the plot and
characters of *Pan Tadeusz* and *Trans-Atlantic*. First, *Pan Tadeusz*
contains a description of a raid by one group of nobles on
another. This way of settling private accounts among frontier
nobility was approved by custom in old Poland. It had its own
rules of honor and its rituals of violence. Such raids are sub-
liminally evoked in Gombrowicz's description of the "sleigh ride"
(*kulig*) which unexpectedly stops at Gonzalez's estate and,
instead of generating violence, dissipates the plans for it. Gombrowicz's use of the word *kulig* makes it clear that he wanted
the scene to be absurd as there can be no sleigh rides in a
tropical climate. The *kulig* scene ends with an outburst of
laughter instead of violence. Second, the secret society to
which the narrator belongs represents a parodic comment on
the secret society in *Pan Tadeusz* of which Robak is an emissary.
In Gombrowicz, no homage is paid to military bravery or the
soldier's attitude. Major Kobrzycki's probity is constantly praised
by the narrator but the latter remains unaffected by it. Third,
the final polonaise in which the characters in *Pan Tadeusz* par-

ticipate and the mood of book twelve of Mickiewicz's epic
(reflected in its title "Let Us Love One Another!"), find an
ironic commentary in the orgy of laughter in which the characters of *Trans-Atlantic* join at the conclusion. Critics have
pointed out that scene by scene and section by section, Gombrowicz's work is a mocking counter-proposal to Mickiewicz's
as well as a critical inquiry into the truths which the romantic
and post-romantic writers imposed upon the reading public.[18]
This does not mean that Gombrowicz set out to defame Mickiewicz's remarkable work. His mocking imitation of Mickiewicz
aims rather at the creation of a new perspective on works which
nostalgically evoke lost innocence and conjure up visions of the
past rather than the present or the future. Nor does Gombrowicz's imitation of *Pan Tadeusz* always take the form of
parody. In some cases, it invokes the same kind of gentle humor
which Mickiewicz occasionally used. For instance, the mock
heroic duel between Major Kobrzycki and the homosexual
Gonzalez is a recasting of the duel between Messrs. Domeyko
and Doweyko in Mickiewicz's work.

In conclusion, Gombrowicz's duel with the recognized masters
of Polish literature does not have as its aim the destruction of
adversaries. It is rather a way of turning the reader's attention
toward an underestimated and largely forgotten period of Polish
culture. At this writing, it cannot yet be determined whether
Trans-Atlantic has influenced Polish prose to the extent the
author sought. It *can* be said that this *gawęda* is a unique work
which sets out to turn the current of Polish literature in a new
and unexpected direction. Few works have been written with
this goal in mind.

VII   Pornografia: *The School for Lying*

Compared to *Trans-Atlantic*, *Pornografia* seems a return to
conventional realism, specifically, to the novel of manners so
popular in Polish literature. For the first time in Gombrowicz's
works, the characters seem to be round rather than flat, the
narration free of neologisms and proceeding in a chronological
manner. However, it would be a mistake to read this work as
a novel of manners or a country novel. Gombrowicz's realism

does not concern manners but attitudes. The seemingly commonplace conversations and exchanges occurring in his novel
are metonyms for the clashes between the subconscious minds
of the characters. Many hints in *Pornografia* alert the reader
to this: Amelia's unexplained death; the bizarre correspondence
between Frederick and Witold; the provocative time and place
of action; and Gombrowicz's own name and surname used as
that of one of the characters. *Pornografia* is a pseudo-realistic
novel whose plot should be viewed as a metonymic reduction
of psychological states to physical images and happenings.

The narrator in *Pornografia* is called "Witold Gombrowicz";
like the author, he is a writer. Also a homosexual and a coward,
he supports himself by running an illegal business during the
Nazi occupation of Poland in World War II. It should be added
that Gombrowicz the author never set foot in Poland during
the war. The plot centers around two middle-aged gentlemen,
Frederick and Witold, who visit the country estate of their
school friend Hippolytus. The time of action is short: one day
in Warsaw and a week in the villages of Powórna and Ruda.
During their stay Frederick and Witold meet Henia and Karol,
both sixteen, who have known each other since childhood and
are good friends. Henia is engaged to Albert, a distinguished
gentleman of the neighboring Ruda. Frederick and Witold become fascinated with the potential sex appeal which Karol and
Henia have for each other. In their yearning for lost youth,
the men decide to reach out to it by "pairing together" the two
youngsters. They desire sexual excitement and, as Frederick
insists, "development." They succeed in stimulating Henia's and
Karol's interest in each other, but the price is a murder which
the two teenagers commit together.

How pornographic is *Pornografia?* Not very much. The plot
outline given above implies more than has been delivered. What
then is *Pornografia* about? According to Gombrowicz's testimony,
it is about the secret and often destructive influence youth has
on the mature. "Youth" reminds "age" of the perpetual immaturity of nature and makes age long for this immaturity. Youth,
with its "unfinishedness," lack of achievement, inferiority and
vague possibilities is, paradoxically, an object of desire and
envy for age. On the surface, age recognizes achievement, real-

ized possibilities, completeness and superiority, but secretly, it desires youth. Maturity is willing to stoop to all kinds of ruses to possess immaturity. It is willing to sacrifice wisdom and experience for what it knows to be unquestionably inferior to it. Youth does not desire age; age desires youth. Thus age's existence is not autonomous; to a large extent, it lives by and for youth.

What is the source of this attraction? Youth has an appearance of beauty, the mainspring of its power over age. Is our concept of beauty, then, somehow connected with inferiority and immaturity? In *A Kind of Testament* Gombrowicz reminisces on how he arrived at these intuitions. When he landed in Argentina in 1939, suddenly to become a man without position or place in society, he as a result gravitated toward the young rather than the mature and well established. He himself looked young and easily passed for a man in his twenties. While thus successfully courting youth, he began to realize that he was only doing openly what others did secretly. In spite of the amenities of age, *they* wanted to look young, be recognized as young and be approved of by the young. Is man, then, "suspended between God and youth," between desire for superiority and lust for inferiority? Is beauty inevitably linked with inferiority, unrealized possibilities and lack of experience?

Gombrowicz investigates these intuitions through the character called Frederick, a refined intellectual thrown into the midst of the Nazi occupation of Poland in the 1940s. At the beginning of the novel he is the silent and ceremonious gentleman who visits the apartment of a Warsaw family as artistically-minded as himself. A discussion about "God, art, the people and the proletariat" goes on while he remains silent. When asked about the purpose of his visit, he answers succinctly: "Eva told me that Pientak often comes here, so I looked in because I got four rabbit skins and a leather sole to sell." This combination of artistic interests and survivor mentality is an ironic echo of Jerzy Andrzejewski's *Ashes and Diamonds* where the concerns of the same generation of characters revolve exclusively around political issues and attitudes.

Perhaps the harsh necessity of dealing in leather soles to survive causes "the junk rooms" of Frederick's mind to open up so daringly. Perhaps, were it not for this, the two friends would not become so influenced by youth and would not engage in the pursuit of the second-rate and the ridiculous. The time of action suggests that the supreme uncertainty of the war "liberated" and enabled them to put into practice their secret pornographic scheme. The idea of making the two teenagers aware of each other's charms is conceived by both friends at the same time. Without ever saying a word on the topic, they exchange unsigned letters in which they discuss the details of the scheme.

During their visit to Ruda they meet the owner of the estate, Lady Amelia who is Frederick's match in profundity and cultivation. She is venerated by her son, her future daughter-in-law, and her friends and acquaintances. Everyone recognizes her probity and the strength of her character. Yet she dies strangely, after a bizarre fight with a peasant boy whom she has caught stealing food in the pantry. It later becomes apparent that the boy would gladly have escaped if she had allowed him to. She did not, however and instead threw herself on him, bit him, and accidentally stabbed herself with a knife which the boy held in his hand. On her deathbed she likewise behaves strangely, turning to Frederick (who is an atheist) and not to Christ in whom she professed to believe all her life. These actions reveal the "other" Amelia, just as Frederick's pornographic longings reveal the "other" Frederick. The junk rooms of their respective minds are different, but definitely exist, nevertheless. Like all characters in Gombrowicz's writings, Amelia desperately wants to impress others. She stares at Frederick on her deathbed because she wants to show him what the death of a good Catholic is like. She throws herself on the boy because she feels threatened in her superiority by the arrival of an equally profound and yet very different intellect. Her unconscious desire for the touch of a young body surfaces and eventually leads to her death. Frederick wants to impress, too, but in a different way. In spite of his intellectual achievements, he feels unattractive and therefore a failure. He knows that the only way to taste youth again is to associate himself with it in some way. He and Witold work hard to attract the young, and they succeed. At the end of the book, the four of them look deeply into one another's eyes. They are of one mind: the old have been united with the young and through that union, have regained for a moment the beauty the young possess. Gombrowicz put it this way: "Man has two ideals, divinity and youth. He wants to be perfect, immortal, omnipotent. He wants to be God. And he wants to be in full bloom, fresh and pink, always to remain in the ascendant phase of his life—he wants to be young. He aspires to perfection, but he is afraid of it because he knows that it is death. He rejects imperfection, but it attracts him because it is life and beauty."[19]

The secret dependence of Age on Youth of which Gombrowicz speaks generates a system of lying that is pervasive and inevitable. The ambiguity of man's inner life is daily confronted with the rigid world of Form, and tries to hide itself under a variety of masks. There are few novels in world literature in which man's capacity for lying is so profoundly taken into account.

The lying which goes on in *Pornografia* is not Freudian displacement, or rationalizing, or trying to protect one's endangered privacy. It is lying pure and simple—the telling of untruth about a state of affairs at hand, by words or by behavior. Amelia represents a refusal to acknowledge or analyze inconsistencies in one's behavior. Frederick wears a mask all the time. *Pornografia* is a tissue of many lies which the characters constantly offer each other. The narrator, part of it, records his own lies and those of others.

The behavior of Frederick and Amelia provide the most interesting instances of lying. They both take care to appear profound and refined—and are. They respect themselves for their refinement, and expect others to show them respect. Genuinely impressed with each other, they are in some way obviously authentic. Yet their impressive façades hide something less impressive. Frederick's "other face" is revealed when he faces a temporary setback in his pornographic scheme (III, 57), Amelia's, when she loses her self-control in the darkness of the pantry. Frederick is not disturbed either by his lying or the occasional unintentional dislosures of it. He treats both as an obvious part of life. But Amelia is disturbed—and pays a heavy price for it.

Like Frederick, Amelia is "penetratingly, irrevocably conscious . . . unfathomably deep." She exudes an aura of imperturbable self-confidence and honesty. And yet, she does things
which put her unshakeability into question and strongly suggest
that she is well acquainted with lying. It all starts when she
is confronted with Frederick's atheism. While able to cope with
the kind of unbelief which is, at bottom, a search for belief,
Frederick's atheism is not that. It is rather alien and uncontrollable. She cannot accommodate it within the system of ideas which
she needs in order to feel wise and secure. She "loses her balance"
and becomes "dizzy and dumfounded." She knows she is "irrevocably compromised" by revealing her insecurity and immaturity.

The feeling of superiority gone, Amelia now commits one
foolish act after another. She throws herself on a peasant
boy and bites him all over. She manifests a childish desire for
praise when she looks up to Frederick for approval on her deathbed. She dies soon afterwards, and thus has no more opportunity to compromise herself; but her behavior before her death
again indicates that her composure and appearance of having
reached ultimate wisdom were lies. Amelia demonstrates Gombrowicz's belief that all maturity is sham and pretense.

The conspiratorial pimping which goes on in the book is an
extended metaphor for lying, not merely because it has to be done
in secrecy but because of the way in which secrecy is achieved.
Frederick and Witold come to an agreement without words.
Outwardly, they pretend that no agreement has been reached.
Soon Henia and Karol become their accomplices in dissembling.
The young and the old come to a tacit understanding and together
develop a way of masking their intentions. All this takes place
while they engage in ordinary social life with discussions about
family, business matters, and the war.

The appearance of the underground officer Siemian generates
another chain of lying. Siemian, an honored guest at the estate,
also to be murdered by his hosts senses the atmosphere of
double-dealing which surrounds him, but cannot do anything
about it. He once tries to break the chain of lies by revealing
something about himself to the narrator, but his challenge is not
answered. Siemian's death, and every death in *Pornografia* in

fact, is accompanied by lying. The liars may be victims (Albert, who never reveals to those with whom he is intimate the troubled ambiguity of his internal life, and Amelia, who never openly admits her failure to live up to the appearances she has assumed) or the executioners (Frederick, who unexpectedly murders Olek, and Albert, who murders Siemian).

The narrator perceives the discrepancy between the characters' behavior and the state of affairs, but is not disturbed by it. He accepts it as a condition of life to which he willingly contributes. He narrates from the point of view of a person well reconciled to the fact that communication between human beings consists in large measure of attempts to deceive.

Nobody is excessively disturbed when the acts of deception are uncovered. Neither the narrator nor other characters ever blame one another for lying. Lying is fair play to them. In John Fletcher's words, there is a "teasing callousness"[20] about the way *Pornografia* is narrated, a radical absence of a censoring tone, a reversal of the values and attitudes which had traditionally underlain the Polish novel of manners. A fundamental assumption of the narrator is that being a man means to lie, that lying is often necessary for personal development. No voice or event in the story challenges this assumption. At the beginning, the narrator says that the "adventure" he is about to relate is "one of the most fatal ones"; however, this is not a censoring remark, but a perception of the distance which separates his story from other stories told in Polish literature. The author of *Pornografia* obviously wanted to pit his novel against the Polish novel of manners with the latter's invariable acceptance of traditional values. *Pornografia* goes farther than any other work of Gombrowicz in the welcome it extends to twisted ways of human development.

VIII   Cosmos

"For me, *Cosmos* is black . . . something like a black stream, turbulent, full of whirlpools, obstacles and flooded areas, carrying a mass of refuse, and in this stream a besotted man, at the mercy of the waters, trying to decipher and to understand so that he can assemble what he sees into some whole. . . . It is an austere book, and I have less fun in it than in my other works."[21] Gombrowicz's comment is accurate. This slim volume whose action takes place in a conventional middle class setting presents the same unintelligible world which the heroes of Kafka and Beckett confront. The plot consists of humdrum events given an uncanny dimension by the narrator. *Cosmos* (*Kosmos*) is a difficult novel not because the reader cannot figure out "what happened" but because physical happenings are only faint hints of psychological happenings. The latter are not explicitly discussed. They are presented in reduced form, as seemingly unimportant physical facts. Gombrowicz's reductive method here reaches its peak.

The narrator named Witold arrives at the mountain resort of Zakopane to study for his exams at the university. In Zakopane he meets his former classmate Fuchs. Together they rent a room in the house of a retired bank official Leo Wojtys. The house is commonness incarnate: the housewife Kulka with her round-the-clock cooking and cleaning chores, the pretty daughter Lena and her engineer husband Louis, and the poor relative Katasia who helps in the kitchen. Witold and Fuchs develop a relationship similar to Witold's and Frederick's in *Pornografia*: they are both voyeurs pursuing their interests with dedication. Their voyeurism is not only of a sexual nature, for they are also obsessed with things such as cracks in the ceiling they imagine are arrows leading them to a discovery of some secret. Toward the end of the book, the narrator enters a similar relationship with Mr. Leo Wojtys who turns out to be no less obsessed with secrets than his two lodgers.

All the characters in *Cosmos* could be called Mr. or Ms. Average. They are neither intelligent nor stupid, neither rich nor poor. They are physically unattractive, or so the narrator tells us; at the same time, however, he is most interested in the ugliest of them all, the servant Katasia whose face had been disfigured in an automobile accident. The characters carry overwhelming obsessions and fears behind their unprepossessing physiques. Leo and Witold are onanists. Witold and Fuchs are compulsive voyeurs. We are never told what was Louis's obsession, but it must have been a strong one to make him commit suicide. The pettier the character, the pettier the obsession: Lolo and Lula compulsively flaunt their successful marital relationship, and Kulka is obsessed with housekeeping to the exclusion of anything else. Then there are the imagined obsessions: the good-natured Katasia assumes demonic dimensions in the narrator's mind. The cut across her lip repels and attracts him at the same time. To justify his interest to himself he ascribes to her qualities she does not seem to possess. The reader, comparing Katasia's behavior to the narrator's monologue about her finds that the behavior in no way justifies the monologue. Yet a residue of reason to doubt remains. The boundary between reality and possibility is not completely wiped out in *Cosmos* as it is in Robbe-Grillet's *Erasers*, yet the persistence of obsessive interpretations suggests that what is considered real is in fact quite obscure, that man's touchstones are matters of convention and accident. The narrator is obsessed with secret messages and seeks them in the most unlikely places. Is then his narration unreliable? Not at all, suggests Gombrowicz. All characters are similarly obsessed and profoundly ignorant of matters about which they express opinions and pass judgments. Kulka's ignorance of her husband's obsessions is stupendous. Louis's and Leo's discussion about the methods of improving society finds an ironic commentary in the subsequent revelations about the secret intuitions of both characters.

Cosmos is a novel about man's uncomfortable position in the universe. If it dealt only with the anguish of modern man, it would have been merely one of the many Kafkaesque novels; however, the central concern of *Cosmos* is a questioning of man's judgments and opinions about the world. The Wojtys' household as described by the narrator of *Cosmos* is a metonym of the universe as conceived by man. It is an arbitrary universe. Its axioms and premises are chosen by accident; another set of premises would have produced a different picture. There are an infinite number of explanations of what is going on. The reliability of those who furnish the explanations is put to question. They are both ignorant and preoccupied with their own compulsive interests. The two students who arrive at the Wojtys' household can interpret the family and the events around them in any number of ways. They are free to make up any story they want. Gombrowicz emphasizes this point by

making a hanged sparrow the first link in the chain of explanations at which the young men arrive. The sparrow becomes a
reference point by accident. Witold and Fuchs notice the bird
hanging from a tree as they approach the Wojtys' house. Alerted
by the bird, they search for other hanging objects and find a
piece of wood hanging behind the tool shed. Later, Louis tells
them about the hanged chicken he once saw, and Witold
strangles and hangs Lena's cat. The string of hangings is completed by Louis's suicide. The reader can easily imagine the
probable sequence of events. Louis was obsessed by the
phenomenon of hanging, and first hanged the sparrow and then
himself. But Witold and Fuchs form a different idea of the situation. The chain of hangings seems to lead somewhere. Never
mind that one of them was engineered by Witold himself, Fuchs
does not know it, and Witold has become too obsessed with the
idea of hanging to distinguish between real and fabricated evidence. As the hangings multiply, Witold is overpowered with
another obsession, the association between Katasia's mouth
and that of Lena. This generates another chain of absurd thoughts
and behavior. Witold longs to enter these mouths, to put his
finger in them, to spit into them. Mouths and hangings are
linked into a coherent whole in Witold's mind. He is satisfied:
he has found meaning in the universe.

The structure he has built looks improbable from the point of
view of common experience. However, Witold holds on to it
because he assumes that a probable structure is an arbitrary
structure on which many have already agreed. He is aware that
combinations accepted as history are not the only ones in existence. An awareness is mounting that other combinations and
other histories are also possible. Human beings fool themselves
by taking their customary perceptions—shaped by a thousand
contingencies—as the only possible reality. There can be—and
certainly are—other realities. "There are no impossible combinations. . . . All of them are possible" (IV, 150).

Leo Wojtys comes to Witold's help in upholding this view.
He too has a private universe whose reality he never doubts
but which at first seems startlingly impossible to Witold. Leo,
an even more persistent producer of reality than Witold, has
been doing so for years. The universe as conceived by Witold

in the Wojtys' house, ceases to preoccupy him when he returns to Warsaw, whereas Leo remains well entrenched in his private vision of the world. Leo's reality centers around the junk room of his mind with its own rituals, goddesses, sacraments and masses. Leo initiates Witold into the conscious freedom of creating one's own universe. In his conversation with Witold, he most fully expresses Gombrowicz's doubts about the legitimacy of the principles of classification used in human culture. *Cosmos* sends us innumerable signals—we choose a few, ignore others, and rest comfortably in the belief that some form of similitude governs the relations between the world and our verbalization of it. Could it be that our theories and the ways of organizing perceptions into knowledge are about as meaningful as the narrator's way of doing so at the Wojtys' house? These suggestions run parallel to some structuralist thinking about history. There may even be a direct influence since Gombrowicz mentions Michel Foucault in his *Journal* (VIII, 196) and in his 1967 *Commentary* on structuralism (X, 531).

There is an intentional absence of Freudian motifs in *Cosmos*. The narrator does not think in Freudian terms, and the author does not allow events to prove the narrator wrong. Sex in *Cosmos* is an expression of human solitude and an expression of frustration at an inability to communicate with others. The two most important characters are masturbators. The three young married couples who appear in *Cosmos* are either nervously eager to play up their sexual awareness (Lolo and Lula), or perpetually unhappy (Jadeczka and Tolo), or soon to arrive at a tragic end (Louis and Lena). Only Mr. Wojtys is reasonably satisfied with his sex life having created a world centered about masturbation.

Cosmos is the saddest of Gombrowicz's novels. Its author confesses his unbelief in any axiom or premise, any origin other than the human mind. He starts and ends with man, so far agreeing with Nietzsche and the existentialists. He does not, however, stop there but further asserts the nonfeasibility of man's prideful autonomy. In *Cosmos*, autonomy cannot be made into a prideful possession. It amounts in practice to the worship of the individual junk room. Leo Wojtys prospers, but it is a sad prosperity, remote from existentialist awareness and Nietzschean supermanhood. The narrator strives to discover a more universal meaning to the world that surrounds him than what Leo represents; however, he is frustrated in his attempts and wavers: "It is hard to call this . . . incessant joining and falling apart of elements . . . a story" (IV, 146). He does not give up on development and does not fall into despair, but the story he narrates is an indication that his development cannot hope to reach spectacular proportions. His mentor, Leo Wojtys, ends up cultivating his obsessions and fashioning a private world in the midst of incomprehensible and indifferent surroundings.

"I was the first structuralist," Gombrowicz said in the interview for *La Quinzaine Littéraire* in 1967, in the half-mocking and half-boastful tone so characteristic of him. He referred to *Ferdydurke* and *The Marriage*. Even more than these two works, *Cosmos* comes close to being a truly structuralist novel: a closed chain of ideas brought to existence by man's obsession with meaning in the complete darkness that surrounds him.

CHAPTER 5

Journal

THE *Journal* (*Dziennik*) is the most enjoyable of Gombrowicz's works. It is also the longest and most spread-out in time: 750-odd pages written over a period of fourteen years. Gombrowicz published it in installments in *Kultura* where many readers took it to be a nonfictional piece, the diary of a writer who spoke frankly about himself and forms of cultural life around him. Gombrowicz encouraged this kind of reception. In the preface to one of the editions of *Trans-Atlantic*, he denied that the story told in the novel is *his* personal story, and directed those interested in the facts of his life to read the *Journal*.[1]

Even a casual reader, however, easily discovers that the *Journal* is not to be equated with an extended entry in a biographical dictionary. Its speaker is stylized, dressed up to resemble Gombrowicz, but not identical to the writer. He is much more open than authors of journals meant for publication usually are. But still, his frankness is selective. In addition Gombrowicz occasionally reverts to techniques of fiction, recording imaginary conversations between the speaker (named Gombrowicz) and some other person (the imaginary interview for *Die Welt*, VII, 186-89), describing himself in the third person, giving a fictitious account of an event in his life—the entry describing the speaker's trip to Europe after twenty-four years of involuntary exile—which contains excerpts from "Events on H.M.S. Banbury." Sometimes there are two speakers, one being a cool and ironic commentator on the actions of the other, an emotional and insecure person. The two voices are distinguished by the type of print: italics indicate the commentator, and ordinary print, the actor.

These examples indicate that deciding the identity of Gombrowicz's speaker is not a simple matter. He is not Gombrowicz recording spontaneous remarks about matters at hand, yet he obviously is somehow close to the writer. He does not fit into the existing categories of the literary characters, the journalistic persona, or the author addressing his readers, but most closely approximates the voice of an interviewed author who takes his interview seriously.

The speaker then, represents a special case of the reduction of the author's personality. The reduction is undertaken to highlight a cause: the *Journal* as a whole can be likened to the old Polish *zajazd* (raid) of one nobleman on another. Gombrowicz fights for a cause, and he presents all the aspects of himself— emotional, intellectual, factual—which are relevant to this cause. The rest is never mentioned.

What cause does Gombrowicz champion? His purpose here is to demonstrate how the public and private personalities of people differ, how man is formed by the things he himself as well as others say about him. Gombrowicz believed that our perceptions of others, especially public figures, are ridiculously distorted, and set up for himself the task of demonstrating this through an example. The public figure he seeks to demystify is himself, and he performs the task with considerable lack of concern for his own psychological comfort.

The beginning of the *Journal* is a direct attempt to lay bare the pretensions of a writer:

> *Monday.*
> I.
> *Tuesday.*
> I.
> *Wednesday.*
> I.
> *Thursday.*
> I.   (VI, 11)

What follows is a running commentary on cultural, social and political events interspersed with the incidents of self-praise and scheming in the speaker's life. This purposeful baring of the seamy side of the speaker's personality cannot but alert the reader to the fact that "serious" views expressed in the *Journal* may have been refracted by petty concerns of the speaker and so should be approached with scepticism. This method of building up doubt in the reader is characteristic of Gombrowicz. It goes back to the self-deprecatory humor of the Middle Ages and Renaissance, and has been evident in other works of Gombrowicz. It is particularly striking in the *Journal* because of the proximity between the writer and the *Journal's* speaker.

Nowhere in the *Journal* can one find a passage where the speaker tries in all seriousness to present himself to best advantage. He takes great pains not to identify himself with his achievements or slip into the role of a Great Writer. He speaks sarcastically of the Polish poet Julian Tuwim who "specialized in playing the role of Poet from his early youth. He endeavored to appear noble, attentive, alert, magical, arduous, humane, sincere, simple. He played this game from early morning till late evening" (VIII, 184). In contrast, the speaker in the *Journal* says: "I must cultivate Jeleński whose importance in both Polish and French letters is on the increase" (VI, 165). Or, describing his genealogical tree in great detail and with quite a bit of vanity, until in his estimate, the reader is sufficiently infuriated, he adds: "What a tasteless snob this Gombrowicz is!" (VI, 183). Sometimes he reveals thoughts inconsistent with his personality-as-perceived-by-others and as advertised by him: in one of the entries for 1956, he describes an adventure which he once had on Christmas Eve, sitting alone in complete darkness in a country house in South America. The weather was stormy. He got up and, for a lark, raised his hand in an imperial gesture of command. All of a sudden, the storm subsided. He dropped his hand and stood in total silence for a while. Then he raised his hand again and the storm began to rage. He did not play this game for the third time, being afraid to do so. A learned and sober man, Gombrowicz was overcome by fear of magic, one is given to understand. He firmly believed that such experiences must be revealed to destroy the image of the imperturbable public personality he had become for some of his readers. Gombrowicz deplores the rigidity of a modern code of behavior which forbids men of some achievement to show their weaknesses in public. He maintains that at a certain level, everyone is unfinished and immature, yet people who publicly communicate with others pretend that this level of immaturity does not exist in them

Somewhat like Kirillov, though for the sake of another cause, he tries to set up an example and demonstrate that human beings as a rule are not always certain of their views.

The *Journal* gives the reader a sense of intimacy almost impossible to achieve in print. In this sense, it is a pre-Gutenbergian work. It talks to the reader the way a teller of tales talked to his audience in the dim interiors of a medieval chamber. There are hardly any calendar dates in the *Journal*, and daily entries are separated by the notations of the days of the week. Another Slavic writer, Vasily Rozanov, once tried to achieve a similar sense of intimacy in *The Fallen Leaves* (1913-1915). Less concerned with his "I" than philosophical ideas and trivial daily happenings, however, he did not achieve the sense of personal intimacy which pervades Gombrowicz's *Journal*.

At the end of his *Journal*, writer Gombrowicz appears disarmed, his authorial imperturbability destroyed, his sophistication in doubt, his fake certainties openly exposed. The reader realizes that unlike most public figures he meets in life, this particular person is unsure of his views and tentative about his knowledge. The waverings of the personality Gombrowicz conveys in the *Journal* are one of his great literary achievements. The intensity and persistence of his search and the frankness with which he records his setbacks make the *Journal*'s speaker the most memorable of Gombrowicz's characters.

CHAPTER 6

The Language

THE use of the Polish language by Gombrowicz is based on a
profound intuition concerning the desirability or undesirabil-
ity at a certain moment in the development of a language to com-
plicate it or to simplify it. This intuition seems to be a privilege
of writers. People using expository prose possess it to a very
small degree, quickly destroyed by prevailing custom. A piece
of advice writers of expository prose—from high school students
to journalists—hear, is to *write simply*. Manuals advise everyone
to use the most concise and the shortest possible phrases. Teachers cross out what they consider unnecessary verbiage in student
compositions.

A great amount of linguistic perspicacity is needed to challenge the apparently irrefutable wisdom of this advice and
perceive a level of communication to which it does not apply.
Naturally, the authors of writing manuals are right. For expository prose, and sometimes for other kinds, simplicity is best.
But there are situations in literature when excessive simplicity
leads to dryness and impoverishment of a language. Gombrowicz
perceives this danger in Polish literature, and his writings are
an attempt to fight against it.

After World War II, Polish literature had its more or less
successful simplifiers. On the "deep" side, there have been the
poet Zbigniew Herbert and the storyteller Tadeusz Borowski;
on the "shallow" side, Wisława Szymborska, Stanisław Jerzy Lec
and a host of others.

Simple and parable-like language which gained acceptance
in Polish literature after the war had important and profound
sources as well. Writers were almost silenced by bitterness and
a sense of the great injustice which had happened to them per-
sonally and to the country at large. They feared verbiage when

dealing with the tragedies of war, and were skeptical of the
high-sounding phrases of post-romantic patriotism. They had
to resort to dry irony to survive as writers. The prose of Tadeusz
Borowski which dealt with concentration camps or the poetry
of Zbigniew Herbert which recorded his development during
and after the war are, perhaps, the best instances of this
tendency. In fact, the very best in Polish post-war prose had the
mark of simplicity upon it. (Something similar in effect, though
partly different in cause, happened in western Europe in the
writings of Samuel Beckett.)

There is little of this tendency toward dryness and restrained
irony in Gombrowicz. His language is neo-baroque: coarse at
times, rich in adjectives and exclamatory phrases, colorful and
going off on tangents with apparent abandon. It resembles
Rabelais in the abundance of linguistic sources from which it
draws: slang and dialect, standard Polish, Latinisms and neologisms. Among Gombrowicz's immediate predecessors, it resembles the language of the novelist and playwright Stanisław Ignacy
Witkiewicz whose novel *Insatiability* (1930) was an orgy of
words not unlike *Trans-Atlantic*.[1] Gombrowicz's language abounds
in what the Russian formalist Victor Shklovsky called *zatrudn-
enie*, i.e., making it difficult, forcing the reader to stare at the
words longer than he would normally like. Gombrowicz felt
that it was not the right time—not for him in any case—to disci-
pline the Polish literary language into simplicity. It must rather
first be disciplined into apparent chaos, re-learn flexibility to
bend backward, forward and sideways as it once had in the
pre-romantic period. Gombrowicz believed that the roots of
good Polish prose go back to the seventeenth and eighteenth
century, which in Poland meant baroque and late baroque. The
literature of that period was still free of *Weltschmerz* and self-
consciousness; it was joyful and unhampered by rules of pro-
priety or fashion. It was the literature of a people as yet un-
touched by the melancholy and inhibitions of Romanticism.

Gombrowicz's tendency to hold the romantic and realist
period in Polish literature in low esteem shows itself already in
Ferdydurke and reaches a peak in *Trans-Atlantic*. *Cosmos* and
the plays represent a judicious use of baroque devices, and
the *Journal*, discussing it all explicitly, on occasion demonstrates

how to return to the baroque attitude of writing without regard
for proprieties of cultural fashion. On the whole, however, the
Journal is much more restrained in its use of verbal structures
than are the novels and plays.

Gombrowicz mocks the gentility of Polish literary language.
He ridicules the superficial smoothness of style by which some
writers contemporary to him gained the reputation of great
stylists. He makes the aristocratic characters in his works use
peasant dialect and city jargon. As innkeepers, Henry's parents
in *The Marriage* use such forms as *swoi* instead of *swojej*, *moji*
instead of *mojej*, *koński* instead of *końskiej*, etc. This narrowing
of vowels at the end of words often occurs in peasant dialects.[2]
It is likewise common in peasant speech not to distinguish
between the two verbal conjugations and to use the ending
emy for the first person plural where *imy* is used in standard
Polish, e.g., *radziemy, chodziemy*. This peasant form is used
by the narrator in *Trans-Atlantic*. Dialects use voiced con-
sonants where literary language has voiceless ones: *jezdeś*. Again,
this appears in *The Marriage*. In addition, Henry's genteel parents
use city vulgarisms, e.g., *zwędzić* instead of *ukraść* (both are
synonyms of to steal), *za pozwoleństwem* instead of *za poz-
woleniem* (wait a minute), etc. The word "pig" and its derivatives abound in *The Marriage*, and on several occasions they
come in an abundance equal to that of the word "laughter" and
its derivatives in Velimir Khlebnikov's famous poem "Incanta-
tion by Laughter" (1910). Deprived of their upper middle class
language, Henry's parents lose their dignified bearing as well;
in Gombrowicz's design, this serves to prove that "what man
really is" is not immanent but rather arises in the process of
communication.

As indicated in Chapter Four, Gombrowicz's use of dialect
partially coincides with his use of archaisms, since dialects
preserved many features of archaic Polish. Gombrowicz uses
archaic adverbs, verbs, nouns, conjunctions. He uses archaic
spelling of modern nouns and verbs. The forms of verbal conjugation mentioned above exist both in dialects and in seventeenth-century standard Polish. Likewise, the spelling of the
word *piniądze* (*money*), with its narrowing of the vowel in the
first syllable, occurs both in seventeenth-century texts and in

contemporary dialects.[3] Gombrowicz uses it in *Trans-Atlantic*
(II,52). In seventeenth-century texts, pronouns, adjectives and
adverbs are usually placed at the end of a sentence or a phrase:
*towarzysz spod chorągwie mojej, stanęliśmy między folwarkami
cicho.*[4] Gombrowicz has *dalej urzędniczka wyfiokowana, wyczu-
pirowana* (II,27), *na pustce drogi mojej i na polu moim* (II,85).
In contrast, contemporary standard Polish usually puts modifiers
before the words which they modify.

The oscillation between archaic Polish and contemporary uneducated speech is one of the ways in which Gombrowicz
achieves parodic effects. One case, where he points to a con-
junction of peasants and nobility against which both groups
protest in *Trans-Atlantic*, is but a natural stance to Gombrowicz
since, as he says elsewhere, "the roots of the nobility are in the
peasantry." Gombrowicz also parodies the ways of speaking
among various small segments of Polish society. In *The Marriage*,
Henry's father gives a speech which resembles a peasant's rendition of a country sermon. In *Cosmos*, Lolo's and Lula's chatter
bring home the idea that the people who consider themselves
members of the intelligentsia are often more ridiculous than
intelligent. Gombrowicz also makes parodic use of the plot, tone,
and phraseology of two of the best known Polish writers—
Sienkiewicz and Mickiewicz. These parodies were discussed in
chapter four. Romantic poets besides Mickiewicz also get their
share of ironic treatment. When in act three of *The Marriage*
Henry's mother runs onto the stage, she shouts the same words
which the mother of Balladyna, in Słowacki's drama under the
same title, utters when she is led onto the stage in pathetic
circumstances. There is no pathos in Gombrowicz, however;
Henry does not pretend that he does not know his mother (as
did Balladyna), and an ordinary conversation follows.

Among parodic uses one should also list Gombrowicz's device
of mixing different styles of speech in a seemingly absurd way.
This is frequent in the plays, which present the world of royalty
and nobility where one unexpectedly often hears undignified
phraseology and witnesses lower middle class manners. The
king in *Princess Ivona* speaks the language of a city urchin. He
expresses amazement by saying "My, my!" or "You are not
kidding!" His anger is vulgar: "Go to hell!" Curse words are

used by the princes Himalay in *Operetta*. This mixing of the styles of speech achieves a double purpose. First, like the mixing of archaisms and dialect words, it points to the fragility of social hierarchies. Second, it is an ironic echo of the elevated language of Polish romantic plays which all the "Professors Pimko" force-fed Polish youth (such as Gombrowicz) in pre-war years. When Frederick in *Pornografia* writes: "I am a Christ crucified on a sixteen-year-old cross. Bye-bye. We shall see each other at Golgotha. Bye-bye." (III,109)—the objective of the mixing of styles is to emphasize the fragility of maturity and the hypocrisy involved in maintaining the pose of an indomitably mature man. A similar objective has been achieved in Gombrowicz's essay on Dante where Gombrowicz's irreverent use of writing styles made Giusseppe Ungaretti so angry.[5]

Gombrowicz's liberties with grammar and orthography are so numerous that only some of them can be mentioned here.[6] Perhaps the most striking is his habit of emphasizing parts of a sentence not usually emphasized, such as prepositions. He achieves this by seemingly random capitalization of words within a sentence. In Polish, no words are capitalized unless they are proper names. Capitalization of common nouns was occasionally practiced in the seventeenth and eighteenth century when orthographic rules were not as strict as they are today. In his *Journal*, Gombrowicz quotes a seventeenth-century note written by his great-great-grandmother which says: "On his way back, Mr. Szolt is requested to buy two yards of velvet and Ginger" (VIII, 196). It is possible that such family notes inspired Gombrowicz's *Trans-Atlantic* where capitalization is practiced with great skill and persistence. The result is a change in the customary patterns of intonation and emphasis. Capitalization forces the eye to remain on the capitalized word longer than usual; a new sentence rhythm is thus achieved, and through it, a new meaning. Words hardly noticeable before become important. New rhythms are also achieved by unorthodox punctuation, a disregard for customary word order, numerous repetitions of one word on the same page, alliterations (*niewolnictwo niedoksztaltowania*) and occasional wrong spellings (*ruż* instead of *róż* in *Trans-Atlantic*, reminiscent of the pre-war avant-garde *nuż w bżuhu*). Gombrowicz also creates new rhythms while using conventional grammar and spelling. An example is the opening paragraph of *Cosmos* in which the subjects and predicates of the neighboring sentences are unusually dissimilar in number and tense, and a wide variety of grammatical forms is used within the complex clause which begins the paragraph. A long string of nouns which is a part of the same clause further contributes to its original rhythm: *ziemia, koleiny, gruda, błyski ze szklistych, kamyczków, blask . . . domki, płoty, pola, lasy, ta droga . . .* (IV,7). In *Pornografia,* Gombrowicz ends sentences with adverbial participles: *informując, widząc*; or uses incorrect sentence structure: *Czy pan jasno rozumie dobrze*; or he uses verbs requiring a direct object without such an object: *Proszę załatwić.* (These examples come from Frederick's letter to Witold.)

One of the most striking examples of Gombrowicz's linguistic inventiveness are his neologisms. Like those of Velimir Khlebnikov and Julian Tuwim, they are virtually untranslatable. The literal renderings in parenthesis are meant to provide some idea about the direction in which Gombrowicz goes. Thus in *Ferdydurke* there are the famous *pupa, gęba, upupienie* and *przyprawienie gęby* (the fanny, the mug, fitting someone with a fanny or a mug) which are now a part of standard Polish.[7] Among the less known are *niedoświatek* (the unfinished world of unfinished people), *kontrnatura* (counter-nature), *półświetni światowcy* (demi-splendid bon-vivants), *antywariat* (anti-madman).

Only descriptive translations can be given for such neologisms as *bachnie bachem swoim jego Bachnie!* (II, 128). There is no verb *bachać* in Polish, and the whole phrase, with its archaic word order and a capitalization of one verb form, is like a child's rendition of the intentions of the homosexual characters in *Trans-Atlantic.* Similarly, *bembergowanie bembergiem w berg* and further derivatives from the root *berg* which does not exist in Polish, are childlike descriptions of masturbation. In some cases, Gombrowicz resorts to nonsensical language: in *Operetta,* the guests at a party exchange meaningless syllables.

The system of inflections which governs the Polish language yields itself to new usages much more easily than the system of word order which plays a correspondingly crucial role in English. Inflected languages can produce lengthy clauses with numerous subordinate clauses in them more naturally than the languages which have eliminated most of their inflections.[8] Thus Gombrowicz's innovations would sound awkward in English, and accordingly, they have often been eliminated from the translations of his works. However, anyone familiar with Polish readily notices that in spite of the anomalous nature of many of Gombrowicz's words and rhythms, they sound strangely familiar nonetheless. In some cases, Gombrowicz's Polish seems rough, even startling at first, but this reaction is soon replaced by a realization that there is in his works the same joyful celebration of language which can be found in the poems of the futurists written at the beginning of this century. Gombrowicz brings forth the latent structures of language, and activates potentialities of it that have long been lying fallow. His usages—and with them, bits and pieces of his world view—are presently accommodating themselves to a place in contemporary colloquial Polish.

CHAPTER 7

The Rhetoric

GOMBROWICZ'S rhetoric is based on the principle of reduction. Where in regard to language he followed the rule
"the more the better," his way of presenting events and attitudes
could well have had "the less the better" as its motto. His use
of the reductive principle accounts in large measure for the origi-
nality of his writings. From the early short stories to *Cosmos*
written some thirty years later, there is detectable in his works
a persistent tendency to present the intangible in terms of the
tangible, the mental in terms of the physical, and the complex
in terms of the simple. Kenneth Burke calls this an archaicizing
tendency:[1] language presumably developed from the simple to
the complex, from an assigning of names to physical objects and
simple actions, to a finding of names for psychological phenomena
and complex actions. The psychological "emotion" presupposes
physical "motion." One can conceive of a literary presentation
that follows this archaicizing or reductive method. Such a presentation would be primarily concerned with psychological states
and ideas, but it would heavily rely on actions and reactions involving the five senses.[2] A further step would encompass a
gradation of sensual actions: the more primitive senses, those
which human beings share with lower animals, to be favored
at the expense of those which are characteristic of higher animals.
Touch should be most favored being the most universal of
the senses (all animals possess it). And this is precisely what
happens in Gombrowicz, in whose works, touch expresses a
variety of psychological relationships. Touching appears in all
its ramifications, hitting, scratching, caressing, beating, biting,
poking with a finger, putting on clothes, taking them off, teasing,
intruding upon the personal space of someone, firing at one another in a duel, or gesticulating in aggressive ways. Also, Gom-

112

browicz's catch phrases, such as "fitting someone with a mug or a fanny," reduce complex psychological phenomena to a series of physical actions involving touching.

Ferdydurke, for example, is the novel most conspicuously built around the principle of touching. Hatred and sympathy, desires and resentments are presented here in the form of two or more individuals doing something to each other's bodies. Usually such an action is contrary to the wishes of another or not expected by him. Most often, touching is an act of aggression. Johnnie bites Professor Pimko's finger and runs away from him; Pimko holds Johnnie by the hand and strokes his head to express his power over him. The teachers at school "fit their pupils with fannies" to make them childlike, naïve, and easy to control. They also "fit them with mugs": a pupil devastated by the patronizing attitude of his teacher assumes an asinine attitude, and his face changes into a mug. Johnnie's revenge consists in shoving his teachers and patrons into "the wriggling heap"— literally a heap of persons lying on the floor and struggling with one another. The image of "the wriggling heap" ends each of the three parts of *Ferdydurke*: the schoolboys are in it in part one, Pimko and the Youthfuls in part two, and the landlords with their peasants in part three.

The two philosophical tales in *Ferdydurke* are likewise full of touching. The duel between Philifor and Anti-Philifor consists of their firing bullets at the bodies of their female companions who gradually lose their fingers, ears, noses, teeth and other extremities and natural protuberances. The duel had been provoked by the two Professors slapping each other's faces. The events in the Philimor tale are a chain reaction of touching started by a tennis ball which has accidentally hit one of the spectators. The characters react physically to what they think are purposeful actions but are, in fact, only counter reactions to physical movements of others. The tennis player's ball hits a spectator in the neck. The spectator's wife, unable to hit the man who caused her husband's discomfort, hits the man next to her instead. This causes panic, amidst which another spectator jumps at the back of a lady seated in front of him. Others follow suit. Soon all gentlemen mount the backs of their ladies.

This tale presents a broad spectrum of human relationships

as a series of physical manipulations of one body by another. The element of random collision expresses Gombrowicz's view that human contacts are likewise randomly hostile, defensive, or friendly.

The plot of *Trans-Atlantic* is full of touching, licking, scratching, hitting, and assuming of physical postures such as sitting, lying, standing in defiance of, or submission to, someone. Throughout the book, characters perform grotesque gymnastics. Members of the Order of the Silver Spur huddle together in a dark basement; an attempt to break away is punished by driving a spur into the culprit's leg. During a diplomatic reception, the narrator and Gonzalez pace up and down the reception room, expressing their wounded vanity, irritation, and discomfort. In their conversations, characters often refer to the physical world rather than to the world of ideas. When the narrator meets the three partners in the firm where he hopes to find a job, they shout at him: "Scratch me! No, you scratch *me!* Leave him and scratch *me!*" (II, 25–26). They resent one another and each of them wants Witold to pay attention to him alone. Witold would like to oblige since he needs a job. So he is willing to scratch them all.

Touching is often sexual in nature—homosexual to be exact— with the characters who touch each other usually being male. The schoolboys are fond of touching each other in *Ferdydurke*, for example. Gonzalez likes to embrace and kiss other men. The gestures of Gonzalez's servant show his awareness of Ignac's sexual attractiveness. In *Cosmos*, the narrator desires to put his finger into the mouth of two men, Louis and the priest; he manages to satisfy this desire. In *The Marriage*, the Drunkard's threat to touch Henry's father with his finger is overtly homosexual. Heterosexuality has a smaller share of touching. Albertine is awakened sexually by the touch of the pickpocket, and Henia and Karol touch each other's soles in the oddly sensual scene engineered by Frederick.

The sense of taste likewise serves to express a person's psychological characteristics. Leo Wojtys is often described as a methodical eater who expertly squeezes the last drop of pleasure out of his salivary glands. The picnic scene in *Cosmos* during which each character munches and swallows in his or her own

way is used by the narrator as a means to characterize each of
them. The way various characters eat is described in *Pornografia*
and *Ferdydurke* for similar purposes (the dinners with Siemian
and with the Youthfuls). References to eating ("the stale noodles
seasoned with the grease of sin") appear at the beginning of
Trans-Atlantic. The discussion about food and the banquet
which follows are among the central scenes in *Princess Ivona*.
Party nibbling descriptions are a means of characterization in
Operetta. The mouth, the organ of taste, is one of the narrator's
obsessions in *Cosmos*. Lady Amelia in *Pornografia* dies shortly
after having bitten the farmboy apprehended in the pantry.

Conversations about ideas are sometimes reduced to culinary
discussions. At a cocktail party in *Trans-Atlantic*, the narrator
meets a "very important writer" (modelled after Jorge Luis
Borges) and talks to him for a while. During the conversation, the
VIP assumes a patronizing tone which irritates the narrator.
This is conveyed as follows:

[The narrator] 'I do not like butter to be too buttery, grits to be
too gritsy and noodles to be too noodly.'
. . . . [the VIP] 'It has been said here that butter is buttery . . . well,
this is an interesting thought. . . . Unfortunately it had already been
expressed by Sartorius in his *Eclogues*.'
. . . . [the narrator] 'It is not Sartorius but I who is speaking.'
. . . . [the VIP] 'It has been said here that Sartorius is irrelevant to
what is being said here. This is not a bad thought especially when
served in raisin sauce, but unfortunately Mademoiselle de Lespinasse
had already mentioned it in one of her *Letters*.' (II, 38–39)

Gombrowicz's works contain many other reductions which
stand for complex psychic phenomena. In *Trans-Atlantic*, the
ambassador wants to impress the narrator by mouthing patriotic
slogans and boasting of Polish readiness for war. "And then
I fell to my knees," says the narrator periodically (II, 16–17).
This metonym expresses his desire to please the ambassador and
take his place in the pecking order. It also is an ironic echo of
Sienkiewicz's *Trilogy* where falling to one's knees was actually
practiced before ladies and princes and signified genuine admiration and respect. Also in *Trans-Atlantic*, the narrator reflects upon
the beginning of World War II in a way that resembles the

leisurely way of speaking of a small town inhabitant wondering
aloud about some minor and puzzling event: "Something, well,
may be wrong ... something, they say, something is not ..."
(II, 76). The reductions in *Operetta* are even more explicit.
Drawing room conversations are conveyed as series of nonsensical
syllables:

MARCHIONESS: Glooglooglooglooglooglooglooglooglooo!
PRINCE: Me? Say Something? (cautiously) Gooa, gooa?
MARCHIONESS: Glooglooglooot!
Banker. Ploot plat![3]

Cosmos is built around still another form of reduction. As
the title suggests, the novel presents man's perception of the
universe as fragmentary and haphazard. Witold and Fuchs
perceive certain phenomena and connect them together in an
arbitrary fashion. They structure reality in accordance with the
workings of their minds. Whatever escapes their attention is
automatically thrown out of existence. There is no way to
check the correctness of their perceptions or of the mental
structures they piece together on the basis of such perceptions.
They muddle through their lives in perpetual uncertainty, and
out of their uncertainty create history.

There is no vertical transcendence in *Cosmos:* the world does
not "look up" toward its creator. Objects are connected by spatial
or temporal proximity. This proximity leads to the formation
of a long chain of associations starting from the hanged sparrow and absorbing other hanged objects such as a piece of wood,
a cat, a chicken and, finally, a man. Another chain is formed by
the narrator's association of Lena's mouth with the disfigured
mouth of the servant Katasia. The narrator explicitly remarks
that Katasia's mouth "refers him" to Lena's (IV, 36). He arbi-
trarily connects these two chains in his mind so that together
they form a bizarre structure which, as Gombrowicz has suggested in his title, is not an untypical part of the structure
called by men the universe.

These examples indicate that the surface realism of some of
Gombrowicz's works has little to do with the realism of the
nineteenth-century novel. It is a fake realism of parody and

the philosophical tale, not striving directly to represent the world or be "true to life" in naturalistic fashion. This realism does, of course, represent the world, but only by schematizing events and people and reducing them to starkly elementary forms.

Gombrowicz's reductive method differs from another form of metonymic reduction that had been a mainstay of prose fiction in the nineteenth century. Jakobson and Halle have demonstrated that metonymy has been a fundamental method in realistic prose.[4] This nineteenth century metonymy, however, was used to achieve different ends. In nineteenth-century prose, persons and events are described selectively, i.e., only some of their features are mentioned. Obviously, one cannot enumerate all the features of the objects under discussion. This would take too long. The reduction here is of quantity rather than of quality.

In Gombrowicz, the opposite takes place. His reductions are qualitative. Instead of outlining objects, he "deforms" them by not describing them directly but making some other object the center of his description. This second object which shares some structural features with the first, is also much simpler. The relationship between man and his fatherland becomes the Order of the Silver Spur. Man's ideas about the universe are reduced to a chain of petty happenings. The agonies of an inferiority complex become "mugs" and "fannies." The duel of wills between the narrator and the "very important writer" in *Trans-Atlantic* becomes a culinary digression.

The theater of the absurd used the reductive method in very much the same way. In their plays, Beckett and Ionesco reduced human experience to boldly simplistic forms. A similar tendency can be observed in the post-Gombrowicz Polish theater, notably in the plays of Sławomir Mrożek. By and large, the Polish novel before Gombrowicz did not favor this method. From Sienkiewicz through Żeromski to Dąbrowska, it relied on the methods of realism and psychologism with an admixture of romantic ideas and attitudes. Gombrowicz's use of the reductive principle coupled with his flamboyant language, makes him an innovative writer within the context of Polish and European fiction.

CHAPTER 8

Women and Other Trivia

G OMBROWICZ'S prose contains a recurring image of a woman otherwise seldom portrayed in literature. She first appears in "On the Kitchen Stairs," the old-time scullery maid in her most unprepossessing form: fat and flat, with ill-fitting shoes and shapeless legs, with a set of bad teeth, a scarf over her head and a shopping basket in hand. She is like the stone women (*kamennye baby*) of the Russian countryside, the mysteriously appealing female without mind or beauty, an ultimate mother unadorned by civilization. There are actually two such women in "On the Kitchen Stairs"—one named Marysia, an aggregate of other characters from out of the narrator's past experiences—and the other, Czesia, a servant in his home whose uncouth ways and manners he secretly enjoys. Czesia is a monstrosity (*pokraka*), an incarnation of ugliness, clumsiness and stupidity, whereas the narrator is a young civil servant with an aristocratic wife and good prospects for the future. His preferences embarrass him a little; he is also afraid of being discovered and put up to ridicule by his acquaintances. But his passion gets the better of him, and little by little, he teaches the servant how to stand up against his wife in household verbal skirmishes. At a certain point, he hides his wife's wedding ring which the wife then accuses Czesia of stealing. This leads to a scandal. Czesia, enraged by the unjust accusation beats up the narrator's wife.

We recognize Czesia in all the female servants of Gombrowicz's novels. In *Ferdydurke* she is instructed by the narrator to laugh with him at the stupidity of the educated folk—a situation similar to that in "On the Kitchen Stairs." She is reincarnated in Katasia, the good natured servant in *Cosmos*. Katasia is more polished than her coarser counterparts in other novels,

118

but her hideously deformed mouth and the narrator's recurring descriptions of it betray her membership in the group of primitive females who so fascinate many of Gombrowicz's characters. For this obsession, we see, is sometimes transferred to characters other than the narrator. In *Ferdydurke,* Alfred carries on a secret affair with the old peasant woman Józefka. In *Pornografia,* the teenager Karol unexpectedly pulls up an old peasant woman's skirt during an after-dinner walk with the narrator: she was "an old woman, a broad-bottomed old slut with sagging breasts, hideous, rancid and foully decrepit."[1] Unmistakably, she is the same "Czesia" whom we first met in "On the Kitchen Stairs." A long-lasting fascination, indeed, since thirty years separate the first appearance of the archetypal scullery maid from the last.

In comparison to this monumental slut, all other female characters in Gombrowicz have a *déjà vu* appearance. They are easily divided into the worthy matrons (Amelia, Kulka), and the two types of young and pretty girls: the passive one (Isabel in *Ferdydurke* and Lena in *Cosmos*), and the saucy one (Zuta in *Ferdydurke* and Lula in *Cosmos*).[2] Most of the time females play the role of close following "shadows" to the male characters in the latters' struggle for power and search for the meaning of life.

The scullery maid is not, of course, an overtly independent character either. Her existence in the book is totally dependent on the desires, fears, and intuitions of the character fascinated by her. She seldom says anything and her thoughts are never recorded. She is the narrator's creation—we see as much of her as he did, and we engage in the same speculations about her as the narrator makes. However, she stands out as a personality in comparison with other female figures.

What role does the female play in Gombrowicz's fiction? His narrators do not relate well to women. Often, they despise and are bored with them. A conventional love affair with Isabel is the last thing the narrator of *Ferdydurke* wants. When the narrator is interested in a woman, as is the case with Zuta in *Ferdydurke* and Lena in *Cosmos,* his interest is coupled with the feeling that she is well beyond his reach, being either too secure, too satisfied with herself, or too pretty to be available. Zuta responds with contempt to Johnnie's awkward attempts at

befriending her; he knows all the time that his efforts are
doomed to failure; he tries without believing that he will
succeed. In *Cosmos*, he does not even overtly try. The narrator's
boldest step in getting closer to Lena consists of an act of voyeurism. He climbs up a tree and watches her talk to her husband
in their room. In Gombrowicz's fiction, there exists a category of
women forever beyond the reach of the narrator. With masochistic pleasure, he returns to them, but realizes the futility of his
schemes to win them over. He therefore, tries to weaken them
somehow in his imagination—throwing a wingless fly into Zuta's
shoe, strangling Lena's cat, or performing other actions of similar
nature in order to make the objects of his desire a little closer
to the type for whom he feels a genuine affinity such as the
scullery maid.

There is little doubt that the scullery maid is the only kind
of woman with whom Gombrowicz's narrators ever experience
feelings of contentment. In "On the Kitchen Stairs" she is described as the mother earth type (IX, 169). What the narrator
feels for her is "a great timidity and tenderness, coming somewhere from the very depth of my being" (IX, 167). No character in Gombrowicz's books ever approaches another character
with such emotions. The "monstrous female" is the focus of all
the kindness and tenderness that exists in Gombrowicz's world.

Why? Gombrowicz's masochistic characters feel very insecure behind the masks of self-assurance or indifference they
wear in front of others. Their insecurity makes them dismiss
conventional sexual encounters as impossible for them. They
cannot really function within the social circumstances in which
they ostensibly live. They cannot "relate" through any other
level but that of the "junk room." Attraction must be coupled with
disgust or else it is not fully satisfactory.

In Gombrowicz's books, the characters stubbornly avoid
developing warm feelings for one another. A whole spectrum
of human relationships and attitudes is thus missing from his
fiction. "Gombrowicz is a great master of language, but I despise
his world view," one well known Polish intellectual told me
in a conversation. His judgment must have been influenced by
the inability of Gombrowicz's characters to have an affection
for anyone other than shapeless, rough and smelly beings who

command both liking and disgust. This eradication of conventional charms allows the construction of a fictional world where "ordinary" female presence is reduced almost to zero and no milk of human kindness flows. The Czesias and the Katasias monopolize all feelings of camaraderie, sympathy and trust which human beings can have for one another. They stand in the background and do not participate in the plot—but are silently there, nevertheless, creatures of the narrators' "junk rooms" and repulsive beacons of warm human feelings in Gombrowicz's loveless world.

CHAPTER 9

Gombrowicz and Other Writers

GOMBROWICZ has always been an eager commentator on his own life and works. Often his comments are tongue-in-cheek. He enjoyed baiting people, including the well-wishers: this was his way of avoiding compromise. As an "aid" for critics, he once composed a list of writers and philosophers who influenced him. It contains two Polish writers, Mickiewicz and Pasek; one Russian writer, Dostoevsky; several Frenchmen, Montaigne, Rabelais, Jarry and the surrealists; three Englishmen, Shakespeare, Dickens and Chesterton; four Germans, Goethe, Schopenhauer, Nietzsche and Thomas Mann, and one Spaniard, Cervantes (X, 521).

The list and the comment indicate that Gombrowicz was not a follower. It did not bother him that the people he mentioned represented widely dissimilar world views and styles of writing. When he spoke of influence, he meant stimulation: he confessed to being stimulated by writings he never tried to imitate. Some forms of this stimulation have been mentioned throughout this book, especially in chapters four and ten. It would be a sterile exercise to take Gombrowicz's "mentors" one by one and try to find all points of intersection between their works and those of their "pupil." What follows is a selective discussion of the methods Gombrowicz employed in making use of the texts of other writers and the direction he followed when accepting the challenge of other writers' thoughts and inventiveness.

Gombrowicz's standing in the Polish and European literary tradition can best be described by saying that he was anti-romantic and pro-Renaissance. He himself liked to say that he was pro-baroque (many features of French and Italian Renaissance reappeared in Poland in the seventeenth century and merged with the baroque tradition. For him, Baroque meant a lack of inhibition and an ability to see human beings as they are in their daily lives rather than in the moments of exaltation or melancholy. He jocularly claimed that his own roots went back to the so-called Saxon period in Polish history when the nobility enjoyed its golden age (VIII, 15). He enjoyed robust and sometimes brutal humor, the kind displayed in works of François Rabelais. Gombrowicz shared with the baroque and Renaissance writers the idea that literature should not scorn amusement. He was fond of verbal ornamentalism, onomatopeia, and the same mixing of styles which characterized the writings of Polish Baroque. On the other hand, he disliked the "high priest attitude" which characterized members of various twentieth-century literary "isms" and which had its roots in the romantic notion of poet as prophet. Gombrowicz scorns the emotionalism which characterizes some Polish writers preceding him. He is suspicious of pathos and, whenever discerning overconfident reliance on its effects by a certain writer, he parodies the example in his own works. His heroes are never plagued by nineteenth or twentieth-century versions of *Weltschmerz*. Gombrowicz was sceptical of works of contemporary literature presenting a hero superior to the crowd and finally defeated by those less worthy. Characteristically, the common point between his Kraykowski and Dostoevsky's Man from the Underground is rancor rather than "heightened consciousness."

I *Gombrowicz and Polish Writers*

Having a strong aversion to romantic attitudes and an admiration for baroque ways and customs, Gombrowicz tried in his books to pit the second against the first. In the context of Polish literature, this meant that he tried to "write against" (his own term) many influential writers who had set the tone of Polish literature for generations: Mickiewicz, Słowacki and other romantic poets; Sienkiewicz and other neo-romantics ostensibly belonging to the period of realistic prose; and also some of Gombrowicz's contemporaries still addicted to the romantic celebration of the self. To fight this formidable army of adversaries singlehandedly was no small task. Gombrowicz, however, found his allies in the seventeenth-century diarist Jan

Chryzostom Pasek, in those writers who used the *gawęda*
genre and in such writers of Polish Renaissance as Mikołaj Rej.
Armed with his convictions and some models from the past,
he began his campaign against those parts of Polish literary
tradition deeply disturbing to him.

The first battle was fought in *Ferdydurke*. Part one of this
novel is dominated by Professor Pimko who is a caricature of
the didactic tendencies of Polish post-romantic literature and
criticism. According to Gombrowicz, the likes of Pimko con-
centrated on the weakest and least interesting features of such
poets as Słowacki and Mickiewicz, and thus made them appear
infantile even to the schoolboys whom they were supposed to
inspire. They adopted the romantic pathos so characteristic of
Słowacki in their own commentaries on literature. This pathos
is of dubious value even in its natural milieu, i.e., romantic
poetry. In the teachings of Professor Pimko, it appears ridiculous as does the neo-positivist (or, for Gombrowicz, post-
romantic) jargon used in the house of the Youthfuls. This
jargon is an echo of the "social" novels of Stefan Żeromski
who combined romantic emotionalism, positivist social zeal and
some modernist tendencies.

Chronologically, the peak of Gombrowicz's "campaign" against
Polish literature occurred in the early 1950s when *Trans-Atlantic*
and *The Marriage* were published, and when Gombrowicz's
literary manifesto, the essay entitled "Sienkiewicz" appeared in
Kultura. At that time, Henryk Sienkiewicz was Gombrowicz's
ostensible target. His duel with Sienkiewicz is, perhaps, the
best example of his way of utilizing native and foreign literary
traditions.

In many ways, *Pornografia* is a parody of Sienkiewicz's *Deluge*.
Both take place in occupied Poland, *The Deluge* in seventeenth-
century Poland overrun by the Swedes; and *Pornografia* in
twentieth-century Poland conquered by the Nazis.[1] The central
motif of *The Deluge* is the fight against the enemy. Everyone
engages in it and selfless sacrifices are freely made. *Pornografia*
deals with this matter rather nonchalantly. Though the time of
action is mentioned at the beginning of the novel, the action
itself revolves around problems very remote from the problem
of national survival. What is more, *Pornografia* portrays an under-

ground officer who decides for fear of his life to get out of the fight. As Gombrowicz emphasizes in the preface, he did not intend to discredit the underground army (*Armia Krajowa*)—which was no less heroic in the 1940s than the seventeenth-century society described by Sienkiewicz. Gombrowicz introduces the cowardly commander "because such were the demands of composition." He was composing an ironic answer to Sienkiewicz's treatment of war, and so demonstrated that, apart from military struggle, other conflicts and other concerns could have been present in the minds of the people during the war years—in fact, most likely, were. It should be added that there was not a single Polish novel dealing with World War II which did not concentrate either on the sufferings or the heroism of the population. It was daring of Gombrowicz to break this tradition. He did so at the risk of greatly undermining his acceptability as a writer.

While in *The Deluge* the faithless and irresponsible Kmicic redeems himself in the eyes of his fiancée and those of the reader by virtuously defending the town of Jasna Góra and by rescuing those whom he once offended (thereby winning the hand of his beloved Oleńka), in *Pornografia* sexual promiscuity prevents the marriage between Albert and Henia. Furthermore, the promiscuity here is of a kind Sienkiewicz's heroes would not even have been able to comprehend. When Henia's and Albert's engagement is first announced, it appears to be very much in the tradition of Sienkiewicz's novels. A chaste maiden from a distinguished country manor is affiancéed to a gentleman from a neighboring manor. It turns out, however, that Henia has had adventures with soldiers and that her views on sexual matters would make Sienkiewicz's heroines faint.

The virtue of older women is also put to doubt. The stalwart matron of yesteryear Amelia, reminiscent of Sienkiewicz's Princess Griselda under whose patronage many young ladies lived, dies in circumstances which, as the narrator suggests, had better remain obscure. Nor are gentlemen to be trusted. The two men who visit the country manor at Powórna are greeted with the same old-time hospitality extended to seventeenth-century warriors who occasionally visited the homesteads of their friends in the country or who rescued ladies threatened by foreign invaders. Frederick and Witold, however, turn out to be lewd homosexuals who complete the process of corruption of the fictional society.

In *Pornografia*, Gombrowicz creates a world which exemplifies Fyodor Karamazov's saying that, "All people live in dirt, but secretly." This world is diametrically opposed to the world of Sienkiewicz. The principal heroes of *The Deluge* are so pure, simple, and righteous that they have no need for any secret life at all—indeed, they do not have any. Gombrowicz created a Mr. Hyde to Sienkiewicz's Dr. Jekyll, less to discredit Sienkiewicz than to provide an alternate point of view on him that was necessary in the dialectic of literary development.

Both Sienkiewicz and Gombrowicz used the same seventeenth-century writer, Jan Chryzostom Pasek, as a source of linguistic inspiration. Pasek was a nobleman of rather narrow mental horizons but remarkable narrative talent. His *Memoirs*, discovered and published in the nineteenth century, have since become popular reading among literary-minded Poles. Pasek's tone resembles the tone of the *gawęda*. If he had written about fictitious heroes rather than about his own life, his work could have been considered the first *gawęda* in Polish literature.

Sienkiewicz and Gombrowicz make very different use of Pasek. Outwardly, Sienkiewicz strives to preserve Pasek's vision of the world. However, he refined and beautified it considerably, and he did not alert the reader to this by making his narrator a much more perspicacious person than his characters. On the one hand, the heroes of *The Deluge*, and of the entire *Trilogy* of which *The Deluge* is a part, share mental horizons with Pasek and his comrades in arms. Kmicic's excesses in his native Lithuania resemble Pasek's brawls and battles. Zagłoba's humor would be understandable to Pasek. The characters in *The Trilogy* are fond of using Latin quotations; Pasek's *Memoirs* is studded with them also. Finally, Pasek's social stratum which represents that sector of the nobility who spent most of their lives in the army reappears in *The Trilogy*. On the other hand, Sienkiewicz's heroes play up to nineteenth-century sensitivity and imagination, thinking, behaving and speaking in a way that would find ready response among nineteenth-century readers brought up

on romantic literature which in Poland combined patriotism
with nostalgia for the past.

Gombrowicz treated the material with which Pasek provided
him differently. He sympathized with Pasek's courage to be his
own imperfect self, and strove to endow his narrator and his
characters with the same fortitude. He also used Pasek's vocabulary and imagery which by his time however, had also acquired
the mark of Sienkiewicz. He, therefore, put all he absorbed to
parodic use. Where Sienkiewicz attempts to be beautiful, Gombrowicz tries to be scandalizing. Where Pasek and Zagłoba
brag, Gombrowicz plays *schlemiel*. Gombrowicz's duels, gal-
loping horses and sleigh rides are meant to be farcical—in
Sienkiewicz, they symbolize bravery, tragedy or joyful celebration. The openness to experience which Gonzalez recommends
and the occupations in which he engages would never even
occur to those of Sienkiewicz's heroes who also were com-
mitting "excesses." Quotations from Latin are replaced by
curse words (g . . . rz, II, 19), and archaic vocabulary is blended
with contemporary dialects (*Tomasz na boku śliwki ji* (II, 117);
*Dopraszam się łaski JWPanie, ale bardzo mnie wstydno . . . Ja
tu zara trochi Pochodzę* . . . (II, 19). Whereas Sienkiewicz's
world is inhabited only by nobility, Gombrowicz mixes social
classes in such a way that conflicts based on different upbring-
ing occur. In Sienkiewicz, the world view, social classes, language and action never clash; things happen according to the
stereotypical notions of how things should happen in a certain
milieu and at a certain time. *Trans-Atlantic* is full of fights
caused by differences in social background and world view.
People of different mental horizons provide ironic comment on
one another. In doing so, they also provide an ironic perspective
on Sienkiewicz and his successors.

Trans-Atlantic is a commentary on Sienkiewicz in one more
way. It is full of exuberance reminiscent of Pasek's world
but which Sienkiewicz's genteel narrative banished. In *The
Trilogy*, the Polish baroque was "fitted with a fanny," polished
and ennobled to fit Sienkiewicz's purpose of "uplifting the
heart." The narrator in *Trans-Atlantic* does not subject himself
to the restraints of didacticism but is willing to take risks and
tell a story about chances taken by himself and others. Some

of his and other characters' pleasures are coarse by contemporary standards, but the narrator does not attempt to dress them up or to gloss them over. He does not play up to the fashions in sensitivity but speaks firmly of his own imperfect personality. The opposite happens in Sienkiewicz whose faceless narrator carefully selects only those details of the characters' lives agreeable to his didactic standards.

Gombrowicz believed that the germ of the Polish literary style was contained in attitudes and modes of being of baroque Poles such as Pasek. In his opinion, Romanticism and its sequels indicated a false turn taken in Polish literature. It was now time, therefore, to turn away from its heritage in favor of returning to what earlier centuries had to offer.

The essay "Sienkiewicz" (1953) is an emphatic expression of similar sentiments. Here Gombrowicz concentrates on the entire *Trilogy* whose action takes place in the seventeenth century when Poland fought against the imperialism of her neighbors while trying to carry out some imperialistic designs of her own. Gombrowicz contends that Sienkiewicz narrated history with a liberal use of poetic license. *The Trilogy* is a perfect embodiment of the legend every nation creates for itself but which only partly corresponds to the actual state of affairs. In Sienkiewicz's defense, it should be said that he wrote *The Trilogy* at a time when the Poles needed a work of literature around which they could rally as they fought to maintain national unity while being divided by three superpowers of nineteenth-century Europe. However, having failed in two major uprisings and suffering reduction in status to second-rate citizens within the empires of which they were part, the Poles were also "ready" uncritically to accept Sienkiewicz's vision of "Poland, the beautiful and the brave."

The situation was different in Gombrowicz's time. National survival was no longer a question. Poland obviously had survived. For readers like Gombrowicz, all the artistic deficiencies of Sienkiewicz suddenly became apparent: his inability to distinguish between prettiness and virtue; his presentation of human choices as basically simple; his tendency to cover up the ugliness of life. Like Fennimore Cooper's, Sienkiewicz's heroines always wear freshly pressed dresses and never perspire.

His heroes always engage in grandiose, worthy pursuits and are immune to petty concerns.

Sienkiewicz is a master in conjuring up this beautified and unreal world. According to Gombrowicz, he is a second-rate writer who performs so powerfully in the area of the mediocre that he deserves to be called a "powerful genius." Gombrowicz compares Sienkiewicz's art to the skill of a beautician who rubs and scrubs and paints the face in order to make it pretty. Similarly, in such novels as *With Fire and Sword, The Deluge* and *Pan Wołodyjowski*, Sienkiewicz rubbed and scrubbed the national countenance until all the blemishes and imperfections disappeared and only pure beauty remained. This kind of beauty, however, is untrue to life. It is Sunday rather than weekday beauty, so perfect and innocent it does not fit well on a nation. By refusing to recognize the value of beauty resulting from experience, Sienkiewicz must ultimately be considered hypocritical. Gombrowicz contends that Sienkiewicz's novels are the Polish daydream in the same sense in which *Gone with the Wind* has become the American South's mythic self-image. He counsels the Poles to establish a distance between Sienkiewicz's art and themselves, instead of identifying directly with it.

Gombrowicz in his passionate polemic exaggerated. *The Trilogy* is by no means so simplistically put together as he suggested. In particular, its last section, *Pan Wołodyjowski*, all but converts the work from the historical novel that has created a national legend, to a novel-tragedy.[2] Gombrowicz does not consider Sienkiewicz's occasional departure from the art of simplification, but speaks only of those features of his adversary's art which in his opinion exert a negative influence on Polish literary taste. This criticism, however, was long overdue. Even though Gombrowicz was not the first to notice Sienkiewicz's weaknesses—the critic Stanisław Brzozowski did before him—he was the first to make a popular appeal against him. Gombrowicz's arguments are now widely known among Poles even marginally interested in literary matters, whereas Brzozowski's reasonings remain the property of a narrow intellectual circle alone.[3]

After "Sienkiewicz," Gombrowicz continued his opposition to

post-romantic Polish literature. After Sienkiewicz, Żeromski, Wyspiański, Przybyszewski, and Kasprowicz come under attack. Textbooks of literary history maintain that these writers ushered new trends into Polish literature; Gombrowicz says that they all wrote in the tradition of Sienkiewicz. Żeromski's mixture of eroticism and patriotism is ill-conceived, the two themes not mixing. Wyspiański's dramas are artificial in their monumentality. The demonism of Przybyszewski comes close to being *kitsch*. Kasprowicz was a pseudo-peasant and his poetry was pretentious in its allegedly rustic tone (VI, 199–207). In all these cases Gombrowicz sees the same lack of authenticity and the same inability squarely to face reality which appears in the novels of Sienkiewicz.

In thus commenting on those writers who perpetuated the romantic attitude and led Polish literature into an impasse, Gombrowicz indirectly attacked the Polish poet whom no one dared to attack for decades: Adam Mickiewicz, a fact not clear to readers of these polemics which kept appearing in *Kultura* in the 1950s and 1960s. Today, when Gombrowicz's work has become a unity, his daring attempt to stand up against the most influential figure in Polish letters is readily noticed.[4]

Nibbles at Mickiewicz were already taken in *Ferdydurke*. In Pimko's lecture to little Johnnie, Mickiewicz's name is mentioned and his poetry is parodied (I, 20). The Słowacki-Mickiewicz conflict is made fun of in the Philifor tale where in connection with the impending duel, Professor Philifor quotes the ending to *Beniowski* where Słowacki expressed the hope that future generations would grant him victory over his adversary (I, 103). But these are small jibes compared to the use made of Mickiewicz's *Pan Tadeusz* in *Trans-Atlantic*. As has been argued in chapter four, the two works are parallel in many ways. However, while the characters and their surroundings were presented in *Pan Tadeusz* with love, in *Trans-Atlantic* they are made fun of. The polonaise which ends *Pan Tadeusz* is changed into an outburst of laughter in *Trans-Atlantic*. This laughter signals an ability of Gombrowicz's characters to treat their own convictions and desires with a measure of scepticism. In Gombrowicz's view, this attitude is superior to the one of unquestioned admiration and nostalgia for the past presented

in *Pan Tadeusz*. In a recent article on *Trans-Atlantic*, Constantin
Jeleński put it even more emphatically: "Gombrowicz decided
to go against the current of time. He wanted to steal Mickiewicz's
baby and leave his own peculiar work at the doorstep of Polish
literature. He believed his novel to be the kind of work in which
Sarmatian Baroque could have culminated . . . The reason it
did not . . . was the appearance of *Pan Tadeusz* and the vision
of conventional and virtuous beauty which this epic poem
contained."[5] Jeleński suggests that the central point of *Trans-
Atlantic* is not the last dance (which is the peasant mazurka
parodying Mickiewicz's aristocratic polonaise), but the scene
in which the narrator meditates upon the young boy Ignac:
"And so I stood in front of him at Night (the match went off),
and I invoked the Night, Darkness and Creativity. I pushed
him into the Night and away from his father's house. Oh, the
Night, the Night, the Night!" (II, 122).

Gombrowicz's comments on Polish writers and his way of
using their works in his own indicate that he attempted to
change the way in which tradition operated in Polish literature.
He favored a criticism of tradition rather than a submission
to it; parody rather than eulogy. Gombrowicz realized that following immediate literary predecessors usually leads to short-
term success and long-term failure, and that creativity is best
nourished by turning to forgotten literary ancestors and divorc-
ing oneself from one's teachers and contemporaries. He correctly
perceived that a great deal of pre-World War II Polish poetry
and prose limited itself to refining and polishing attitudes out
of the recent past, and that many talented Polish writers took a
dead end road. His parodic zeal in regard to the acclaimed
masterpieces of his native literature cannot be compared to
that of any other writer. In the dialectic of literary development
he was a powerful and much needed agent of negation.

II *Gombrowicz and Dostoevsky*

Gombrowicz rebelled not only against Polish literature but
also against those foreign writers whom he admired but with
whom he profoundly disagreed. Foremost among those writers
who evoked his parodic tribute was Dostoevsky. Owing to the

adversary's tremendous reputation, Gombrowicz's "attack" was elaborately camouflaged and is easy to miss at first reading. However, the regularity with which minor details from *The Brothers Karamazov* reappear in *Ferdydurke* leads to the conclusion that we face design rather than coincidence.

What is the reason for Gombrowicz's dispute with Dostoevsky? It seems that the reason lies at the very heart of Gombrowicz's artistic objectives. In his books, he deals with a part of man seldom taken seriously by Dostoevsky—something that comes to the fore *between* moments of crisis, of unusual experience, of deep probing and stock-taking; a part accounting for the triviality of daily human concerns rather than the extraordinary feats of which man is sometimes capable. The pettiness of human existence is at the core of Gombrowicz's interests. He sees in man a being that is unfinished and incomplete most of the time. Dostoevsky, to the contrary, deals with men and women in the exceptional moments of their lives. His characters are generally shown only in those moments when their mental energy is at its peak and when they are most capable of thinking, feeling, and acting. Everyone is an aristocrat in this world in the sense that he or she is always tormented by "accursed problems" rather than small everyday cares. Gombrowicz's parody in *Ferdydurke* consists in baring the element of phoniness in this aristocratism. He fills in the gaps in Dostoevsky's large design by showing the petty dimension of human life which Dostoevsky does not deign to notice.

What are the details of this parody in *Ferdydurke*? Gombrowicz concentrates on two secondary motifs in *The Brothers Karamazov* concerning the children for one, and the noble peasant for the other. Both are parodied within the main plot line of Gombrowicz's novel. The plot of *Ferdydurke* revolves around a group of schoolboys who in many respects resemble the schoolboys from *The Brothers Karamazov*, being pranksters given to occasional displays of bravery and recklessness before their peers. They are very sensitive to the opinions others have of them, and some of them are fairly malicious. They like to compose ditties about their teachers or to embarrass them in some other way. Part one of *Ferdydurke* is full of schoolboys' pranks—and there is no need to remind anyone who has read the novel, about the variety of jokes it contains. But the readers of *The Brothers Karamazov* often become so involved with the book's major themes that they forget about such displays of teenage temperament as the little poem composed by the classmates of Kolya and Ilyusha about one of their teachers: "Astounding news has reached the class: Kolbasnikov has been an ass."[6] This could have been excerpted from *Ferdydurke*, just as some of the classroom scenes there could have been inserted into the descriptions of the pranks played by the boys in *The Brothers Karamazov*.

There is, however, a crucial difference between Dostoevsky's and Gombrowicz's schoolboys. The first undergo a miraculous change for the better within a very short span of time, whereas the second remain their imperfect, rancorous and vain selves throughout the novel. Dostoevsky's boys are first introduced as self-conscious and pitiless toward peers, animals, and adults. At the end of the novel, however, they become innocent souls ready to defend noble ideals under the leadership of Alesha. The "before" and "after" are particularly striking in regard to Kolya and Ilyusha. Before: during one of his walks Kolya notices a goose picking at the grains of wheat under a cart. The goose's neck is so close to the wheel that it is enough to turn the wheel a little to behead the bird. No sooner is this thought than done, and Kolya has a good laugh at the neatness of the whole operation and the anger of the peasant who owns the goose. Another example is Ilyusha's throwing the hungry dog (his favorite, we are told) a piece of bread in which a pin is hidden. The dog swallows the pin and runs away howling with pain. After: Kolya nurses Ilyusha's dog to health, and Ilyusha forgives the boys who used to throw stones at him and humiliate him and his father.

These overly facile transformations did not seem convincing to Gombrowicz. Indeed, the boys do change from little devils to little angels a trifle too quickly. Their dark side is too easily dismissed; their light side too easily called to life. God and the devil are here, but do not confront each other as they do in Dostoevsky's mature characters; instead, they deliver little soliloquies as the boys, alternatively, torture the dog and the goose, and swear to Alesha that they will be virtuous forever.

Gombrowicz's similar group of boys is divided into two antagonistic camps: the virtuous one headed by Siphon, and the nasty one headed by Mientus. Siphon is a caricature of Alesha Karamazov. Like Alesha, he inspires others with noble sentiments and, also like Alesha, is "violated" by the nasty boys at school who having brought him down to the floor hold him there and shout obscenities into his ears until he becomes well informed about the relationship between the sexes. (A similar scene occurs at the beginning of *The Brothers Karamazov* where Alesha's schooldays are described.) Gombrowicz's "virtuous" boys, however, are ridiculous; they mouth platitudes they do not understand, and have little in common with virtue. The "nasty" boys are much more convincing. They fight the never-ending battle of pupils against mentors, and embody the spitefulness of immaturity toward what they perceive to be the undeserved power of maturity. They are "green": they know it, do not like it, but remain so, owing to the limits of their life experience.

Gombrowicz's parodic presentation suggests that the boys' nastiness, pranks, docility and submission to Pimko stem from their "greenness" rather than being a manifestation of some profound spiritual struggle. Instead of interpreting immaturity with the help of the ideas too big for the case in question, Gombrowicz keeps conflicts among the schoolboys on the level of ideas the boys are able to comprehend. *Ferdydurke* contends that the world of schoolboys is better suited to represent man's clumsiness and incompleteness than the metaphysical uncertainties Dostoevsky imposes upon it.

In part three of *Ferdydurke* another aspect of human immaturity comes to the fore exemplified by Mientus's desire to "fraternize" with the farmboys. "To the farmboys, Johnnie! Let's run away from the city to the country where the farmboys are!" (I, 192). Mientus hopes that the farmboy is an opposite of the educated folk who live by artificial standards and patronize or are patronized by others instead of just "being themselves." So he and Johnnie run away to the country. The countryside of their dreams is peopled with the bearers of truth not unlike those naturally righteous souls we encounter in Dostoevsky's novels: Zosima's orderly Afanasy, the house servant of the Karamazovs' Grigory or the servant at the Stavrogin estate, Aleksey Egorovich. The real countryside, however, is peopled with persons like Bert, a house servant at the country manor which the boys visit who is humble and submissive, but not with the meekness of the just which is characteristic of Dostoevsky's peasants. In particular, Bert dislikes "fraternizing" with his masters. In his view, the world consists of masters and peasants; the masters are there to slap, and the peasants to be slapped. He approves of this arrangement even though he harbors spite-fulness against the masters. The only occasion on which Mientus manages to communicate with Bert has to do with slapping. After many unsuccessful attempts to "fraternize" with Bert, Mientus engages him in a conversation during which the ritual of slap-ping and being slapped is discussed. He asks Bert:

'Does your master slap your face?'
The lad's face lit up, and he exclaimed with rustic delight:
'Slap my face? and 'ow, sir, and 'ow!'
This caused me to leap forward and hit him with all my strength . . . on the left cheek; the blow resounded in the silence like a revolver shot. The lad put his hand to his face, dropped it, and rose to his feet.
'You certainly know 'ow to 'it, sir!' he muttered with respect and admiration.
'Get out!' I shouted at him.
He got out.
'What on earth have you done? . . . groaned Mientus, wringing his hands. 'And I wanted to shake hands with him! And I wanted to shake hands with him!'[7]

Compare this with Zosima's pathetic account of how he, too, used to slap his orderly in the face and how one day remorse for a particularly ferocious slapping overtook him; how he humbly apologized to Afanasy until the latter burst out into tears and the two were reconciled in mutual forgiveness. This slapping and the subsequent "fraternizing" with Afanasy changed Zosima's whole life. He refused to fight a duel, asked for a discharge from the army and became a monk.

The parodic relation between Dostoevsky's and Gombrowicz's peasants consists, then, in the following: both writers create peasant characters who exemplify humility to a very significant degree; what is missing in Gombrowicz is all the values which Dostoevsky's peasants represent in addition to their meekness. Gombrowicz instead looks at this meekness through the eyes of a skeptic, a point of view Dostoevsky never used in this context. Gombrowicz's scrutiny intimates that persons possessed of such meekness cannot at the same time be carriers of all those lofty virtues Dostoevsky imposed upon them; that certain combinations are simply impossible within the human matrix; that righteousness is granted to Dostoevsky's peasants gratuitously; that the world of Zosima's orderlies and of devoted country servants is fantasy rather than reality. If people of such meekness existed, they would be more likely to resemble Bert.

In *Ferdydurke,* Gombrowicz attacks the same utopian paradise which Dostoevsky first exposed in *Notes from the Underground* and which he never ceased to denounce. Dostoevsky did it, however, in a tone equally as solemn as that of his oppotent, Nikolai Chernyshevsky in the latter's novel *What's To Be Done?* Gombrowicz mocks this tone. He mocks both the creators of the idea of the crystal palace and its detractors. *Ferdydurke*—and other of his works as well—argues that utopian paradise is impossible not because man harbors sinister and contradictory drives in his innermost soul—but because man simply amounts to much less than either Chernyshevsky or Dostoevsky think. From time to time, man may engage in the lofty pursuits of which they speak. Most of the time, however, he does not. The basement of the human mind is not, as Dostoevsky believes, full of cosmic spitefulness, but rather full of petty desires and an underlying uncertainty.

Much of what man believes about himself is contradicted by daily preoccupations. In comparison to the world of his own culture, man as an individual is underdeveloped. He does not measure up to the culture he has created. All too often, he prefers *kitsch* to culture. Dostoevsky's answer to Chernyshevsky was to treat man as a metaphysical being; Gombrowicz treats him as a being, by and large, incapable of grandeur. Like Samuel Johnson in *Rasselas,* he reminds his readers that the odds are overwhelmingly in favor of them living uneventful and drab lives rather than participating in extraordinary events and situations. In the words of Gombrowicz's *Journal,* man has too often been presented as inhabiting either the arctic cold or the tropics, whereas in fact it is proper to depict his dwelling place as being the temperate zone. Lofty arguments about man do not take into account what constitutes the bulk of daily human thoughts and actions. Neither metaphysics nor socialist organization are relevant to many of these thoughts and actions. In the words of Dmitri Karamazov, man is a creature in whose heart God and the devil incessantly fight a battle. Gombrowicz ironically contends that much of human life lacks such splendor. In parodying Dostoevsky, his aim has been to deal a blow to what he considered inflated opinions of human beings about their most cherished concerns and interests. In so doing, he practised what he said in the interview quoted at the beginning of this chapter, always writing "against" the writers he admired most.

Summing up, there are hardly any "influences" in Gombrowicz's work in the traditional sense of the word. For Gombrowicz, influence means parody rather than apprenticeship. He likes to construct parodic responses to works of literature whose tone is always serious and whose themes are always high-minded. He enjoys baring the secret trivialities of life, thereby undermining at least some of the credibility of his "adversaries." **He** opposes the worship of masterpieces and the attribution of absolute artistic infallibility to them. His parodies which stimulate the reader to further ponder authors parodied thus fulfill a role otherwise ignored by docile imitators.

CHAPTER 10

Gombrowicz's Universe

I The Nietzschean Framework

THE individual's desire for self-assertion and his will to power are features generally recognized in Gombrowicz's writings. In a perceptive essay on Gombrowicz, Jan Demboróg maintains that Gombrowicz's style, thinking and perception of the world have been shaped to a large extent by Friedrich Nietzsche.[1] Gombrowicz's works disregard the individual's obligations to society and concentrate on his fight for psychological well-being. Gombrowicz himself seems to perceive relations between men as basically hostile, one life trying to eliminate another in order to come to full flower. This is not merely a Darwinian fight for survival. The stake is not just survival but the development of such qualities as creativity and refinement. Nietzsche is often mentioned in Gombrowicz's *Journal*. Even though this usually occurs in a polemical context, the influence is apparent for one does not generally argue with a person if that person's views are of no importance to one's perception of the world. Gombrowicz himself admits in an interview that Nietzsche exerted an influence on him (X, 521). A comprehensive discussion of Gombrowicz's works has to take Nietzsche into account. Even though the two are ultimately poles apart in their vision of man, they do indeed share some intuitions about the human predicament.

Nietzsche is often remembered today for *Thus Spoke Zarathustra*, the work which most fully articulates the goals of future man and the proper methods for their attainment. The spiritual attitude which this work so eloquently advocates is that of a striving to overcome oneself. When successfully liberated from pettiness, the striver may at last concentrate on creativity and wisdom. He is then infinitely removed from the

138

gnomes in the "murky shop ... full of impotence which cannot retaliate,"[2] forgers of false ideas described in *The Genealogy of Morals*. The joy he thereby achieves cannot be compared
to any other. He is fully autonomous and lives in the austere
but fertile land of creativity.

In the less well remembered *The Genealogy of Morals*,
Nietzsche describes an opposite kind of man. Here he identifies
an attitude for which he uses the French word *ressentiment*.[3]
It is the attitude of the Underground Man who chews over real
and imaginary offenses he has experienced in his past, and who
on this basis construes notions of good and evil, right and wrong.
He, being the insulted and the injured, is obviously in the right.
Those stronger than he, the insulters and the injurers, are in
the wrong. In thus calling on the *other* to account for a great deal
of what goes on in the consciousness of individuals, Nietzsche
is a precursor of modern psychology. He himself, however, sought
to limit this overwhelming dependence on others only to certain
types of men, those in whose life *ressentiment* plays an important role. The Zarathustras of this world, or even the disciples
of Zarathustras, are granted the possibility of autonomous
existence.

Gombrowicz's artistic world seems situated between the
two poles created by the types of people described, respectively,
in *Thus Spoke Zarathustra* and *The Genealogy of Morals*. His
characters are concerned with either adopting the attitude of
superiority or joining the ranks of those conscious of their inferiority. At the same time, his characters are obsessed with
the will to power. When they yield to another's will, they do so
reluctantly and only after a struggle. Nobody surrenders easily
in Gombrowicz's world. The omnipresence of the struggle for
autonomy is a peculiarity of Gombrowicz's fictional society.
It is not a privilege of the enlightened only, for the least developed ones engage in it with equal vigor. The scullery maids, the
archetypally coarse peasants, the young and the immature fight
for it together with the refined and the sophisticated. The
creatures of *ressentiment* participate in it just as do those in
whose life *ressentiment* does not play a role.

Critics have noticed that in all four novels by Gombrowicz
there appears a character who is the narrator's companion,

stronger and more developed than he, who in many ways "arranges" the action.[4] The respective "stage producers" are Frederick in *Pornografia*, Leo in *Cosmos*, Gonzalez in *Trans-Atlantic*, and Mientus in *Ferdydurke*. The first three (Mientus is too young fully to qualify) can be called Nietzschean in that they devise a way of living which bespeaks wisdom and ability to master the human predicament. Frederick teaches Witold "what it all is about"; Leo Wojtys teaches him how to regard others with amusement and a lack of serious concern; Gonzalez teaches him how to dare to abandon the habit of submission to his superiors; and, on a small scale, Mientus awakens in the narrator the desire to leave the patronizing of Professor Pimko and seek authenticity and freedom elsewhere. These characters not only win their duel of wills but also develop themselves in a way unfamiliar to the narrator. They appear secure in their superior understanding and the narrator recognizes their unassailability. This is perhaps clearest in the case of Frederick whose superiority, beyond any doubt, is felt both by his disciple, Witold, and by his rival, Amelia. He is a great teacher of the meaning of existence. But Leo Wojtys, although less spectacular, is likewise certain of his own wisdom, as is Gonzalez when he argues with the narrator about the best way for Ignac to go. These characters seem free from dependency on others, petty resentments or unresolved conflicts. They have transcended their problems, are creative (Gonzalez, Leo, to some extent Mientus), or creative and capable of sublimating (Frederick). They seem to represent the idea that Nietzschean creativity and a certain kind of sublimation are the best means to rise above the slavish and undeveloped masses.

A whole gallery of Gombrowicz's characters are portrayed in various stages of the struggle for autonomy. Such are the narrators of the four novels who, in addition to participating in the action according to the instructions received from "the stage producers," are exposed—at least once in the course of the novel—to the lectures delivered by the "producers" on the best ways to conduct one's life. Throughout *The Marriage* Henry desperately strives to join this group. Still other characters are primarily creatures of *ressentiment*. Here belong almost all the supporting casts in the plays: the courtiers in *Princess Ivona*, the princes Himalay and their guests in *Operetta,* Henry's parents in *The Marriage.* However, they too manifest the will to power from time to time, not being totally subdued or reconciled to some form of the secular "holy lie." They have not given up striving to gain autonomy and independence from others.

However, are the stage producers truly the masters of life? They teach this mastery to their companions—but are such actions generated by themselves rather than others? A second look at Gombrowicz's "Nietzschean" characters gives the lie to their pose as stage producers, and reveals them to be as dependent on others as Kraykowski's Dancer or some other weakling crushed by fate in an early Gombrowicz story. Frederick does not begin to act until he is confronted with the youthfulness of Henia and Karol. He "comes to life" only when he meets them, after which he begins not only to desire, but also to seek ways to satisfy his desires. So much does he long for the multitude of possibilities which youth possesses that he engages full time in a scheme that will bring him closer to the pair of youngsters—and, hopefully, to their youthful potentialities. Henia and Karol possess what Frederick does not: beauty, ignorance, curiosity that has not yet been satisfied. Frederick knows better than to believe these qualities can ever be reconciled with his wisdom; but, when he encounters them in other human beings, he cannot resist their appeal and wants to experience them again. He can, however, do so only vicariously, through Henia and Karol. To accomplish this he stoops to a humiliating scheme. He, being the sage to whom Lady Amelia has surrendered her wisdom, becomes exposed as one ridiculously dependent on two teenagers. Having reached the level where he is immune to competition with other refined beings, he remains vulnerable at another, lower level. In a sense, Henia and Karol manage him rather than he them. One might argue that the young people are unconscious of their role and therefore unworthy of the name of stage producers. It cannot be denied, however, that Frederick does not deserve the label either. Consciously submitting to the charm of youth, he arranges his life at Powórna in such a way as to follow youth at any price. His dependence is not as overt as that of Kraykowski's Dancer, but no less real for all of that.

which René Girard gave the name of mediated desire. Girard's argument runs as follows:

In *Deceit, Desire and the Novel* Girard examines some of the major European novels and finds a certain tendency which seems linked to the development of the novel as genre. He uses the term "mediated desire" to describe the attitude of those characters whose desires do not travel directly *to* objects but pass *through* another person, a "mediator" whose presence is the real cause of desire. Characters "borrow their desires from the Other in a movement which is so fundamental and primitive that they completely confuse it with the will to be Oneself."[6] Girard demonstrates the omnipresence of this confusion in romantic and post-romantic novels where characters are one another's mediators and where autonomous desire ceases to exist.

One may argue that the phenomenon Girard describes is even more universal than he wishes to claim. It certainly is amply present in Gombrowicz whose characters are acutely aware of the presence of others. Their awareness manifests itself as both a will to conquer and the Nietzschean *ressentiment*. But Nietzsche's ideas are too rigid to describe the full range of dependence on others which Gombrowicz's works demonstrate: Girard's framework is more appropriate. We encounter in Gombrowicz not only overt resentment but also other forms of the Other's influence. Here characters desire something, only because others desire the same; they act to impress others or defend themselves from them. Baron Firulet and Prince Himalay desire Albertine not because she is pretty and thus capable of generating desire, but because she can be dressed up in splendid clothes and shown to others, thus adding to the glory of her conquerors. Henry's father wants to be king to protect himself from contempt and ridicule, not because he desires kingship in itself. The courtiers in *Princess Ivona* never cease comparing their positions at the court with one another's, so as to size themselves up. Even such seemingly "self-generated" actions as eating and drinking are often only means to assert oneself vis-à-vis others. "Against whom is Uncle eating this piece of fruit?" wonders the narrator in *Ferdydurke*. Upon reflection, he then exclaims: "Against the servants, of course!" Gombrowicz's characters seem not to have autonomous existence at all. They are incapable of spontaneous desire. Their life goals and the pettiest of their daily actions are more other-oriented than self-oriented. If they desire excellence, it is only in order to elicit reactions from others. In short, even when not overpowered by *ressentiment*, they experience "mediated desire."

It should be added, however, that Gombrowicz's conclusions are different from what Girard perceives to be the common insight of the novelists who portray "mediated desire." Gombrowicz's narrator does not subtly disapprove of what goes on; on the contrary, he accepts it as a feature of life. The reader is not invited by means of situational ironies imperceptible to the narrator to hold a different view. The author and the narrator do not diverge in their assessment of "mediated desire."

II Echoes of a Catholic World View

The duels of wills in Gombrowicz's books produce an impression of being fought by people for whom dueling is an act of dependence on, as well as defiance at, the adversary. For that reason, relationships in Gombrowicz's fictional world are tremendously unstable and attitudes are readily interchangeable. Worms can change into stage producers and vice versa. People with a masterly manner acquire the countenance of slaves when circumstances change; slaves easily acquire the aura of respectability. Victories and defeats are make-believe, occurring on the surface only, leaving the essential immaturity of the characters intact. What does matter is the process of dueling itself. Gombrowicz never tires of pointing out how omnipresent "dueling" is in human life.

To show that the consequences of dueling are relatively unimportant, however, Gombrowicz often ends sections of his novels—or even the whole novel—with an image of "the wriggling heap"—a scene in which the randomness and sham involved in the exercising of power is displayed. *Ferdydurke* ends with the wriggling heap in a literal sense. The masters and the servants lie on the floor trying to extricate themselves from one another's grasp. A similar scene ends the schoolboy part of the novel. In *Trans-Atlantic* the image of the heap is transformed into universal laughter, the characters become paralyzed by it, unable to maintain their positions of dominance or submission.

The image of the heap is one of the most characteristic features of Gombrowicz's novelistic structure. It is the ultimate tearing off of the masks of aggression worn by the adversaries, an admission of the inadvertence of actions allegedly directed toward goals of autonomy and power. Gombrowicz distrusts the idea of maturity and supermanhood, and is sceptical of the aura of sublimation which seems to surround some human beings. He views mankind as perpetually immature and perpetually given to hiding this immaturity. In view of this, any comparison of his vision of mankind to Nietzsche's or Schopenhauer's eventually breaks down, since both these thinkers credit humanity with far too much seriousness and far too great a desire to sublimate. In Gombrowicz's world, human beings often fake having sublimated their desires while remaining sensitive to stimuli at a level which they do not even acknowledge. Their high culture and the power they struggle so hard to achieve, will only mask the unmendable incompleteness which shows itself in their inability to act independently and in their need to react to others rather than relying on self-generated action.

There exists a striking convergence between the way Gombrowicz's characters behave and their creator's early philosophical affiliations. Gombrowicz's view on man resembles the Catholic Church's, with transcendency removed. He was brought up in the Catholic doctrine, turned away from it in his teenage years, and never returned to it—or so he thought. However, his insistence on man's lack of self-sufficiency seems a distorted echo of the Catholic tradition which lays stress upon the individual's dependency on others (the communion of saints). In this respect, Catholicism differs from most branches of Protestantism which stress man's independence and his ability to achieve. (I am dealing here with tendencies rather than with theology since in the arguments of theologians of both sides, dependence and independence may play changing roles.) Gombrowicz was not immune to the philosophical tendencies of his youth. He rejected whatever seemed unwarranted by his understanding of the matter, namely, structured worship of God; but he retained what he perceived as true to life: man's incompleteness masquerading as completeness which he gave a new label—immaturity pretending to be maturity. His insistence on the pervasiveness of the "subculture," the unflagging energy with which he laid bare the pretensions of the seemingly mature characters, bespeak the same humility which characterizes the Catholic world view. In this context it is possible to understand the statement of his longtime friend and confidant Dominique de Roux who said that Gombrowicz was for him "an incarnation of the Christian Middle Ages with their acceptance of royalty and priesthood."[7] De Roux's comment deliberately disregards some other ingredients of Gombrowicz's poetic universe, namely the lack of a divine center and the defiant praise of immaturity. But, it is valuable as it brings into focus an element in Gombrowicz which is often disregarded by those commentators who see in his works a manifestation of egocentric drives and total disregard for whatever lies outside man's selfish interests and desires.

III *Gombrowicz and Modern Psychology*

An important aspect of "reaction to others" in Gombrowicz's works is the necessity which his characters feel to hide their feelings and intentions from one another. In this respect, perfect equality exists among them. The weak and the strong, the leaders and the followers engage in the art of dissembling with similar dedication. Here too they differ from the Nietzschean hero who displays a distaste for double-dealing. The strong man does not lie—being above it. Not so in Gombrowicz. His short stories mark the beginning of the tendency to dissemble: here, one still finds such characters as the outlaw in "The Rat" who act in the open, either in panic or defiantly, as the case may be—but without using the additional weapon of the lie. In the longer works, characters are seasoned duelers who have learned the tricks of successful cheating. They perform actions which catch their adversaries unaware. They say things they do not mean, and do not say what they do mean. Universal secrecy pervades the world in which they live. In this world, it is impossible to be "oneself." Faces become mugs, adults become children, old and resigned men fake enthusiasm and good faith. Frederick is an example of the falsity of verbal and other behavior by Gombrowicz's characters. When the engagement of

Henia and Albert is celebrated, Frederick rises to give a speech. He is an intelligent man and a good orator, yet under the influence of his secret emotions his composure breaks down:

And soon, to the horror of the orator himself, it transpired that his speech was nothing but an effort to distract our attention from the real speech, the speech without words, beyond words and full of a meaning that words could not convey. Through the well phrased commonplaces transpired the very essence of this being; nothing could efface his face, his eyes expressing something implacable—and he, feeling he was becoming atrocious, and therefore dangerous to himself, did everything he could to seem kind and inoffensive, and embarked on a conciliatory, super-natural, arch-Catholic speech about 'the family as a social entity,' 'the national heritage,' and so on. At the same time his disillusioned, implacably present face was a real insult to Amelia and her guests.[8]

A similar revelation is conveyed by means of Frederick's non-verbal behavior. Here too the culprit is his face, usually well prepared to meet the faces it meets. However, under the influence of his emotions, his face occasionally reveals the state of his mind:

The true face of an elderly man is concealed by a secret will power, trying to mask the decay, or at least arrange it in an attractive whole—once disappointment had set in Frederick lost all his charm, all hope and all passion, and his wrinkles spread and crawled over his face like worms on a corpse. He was abject, humbly odious in this submission to his own horror—and his abjection contaminated me to such an extent that my own worms arose, crawled out, climbed up, and polluted my face.[9]

This constant necessity to dissemble makes Gombrowicz's world an artificial one in the sense that it is built on secondary and tertiary meanings of gestures and actions. Few things are natural in this world where the simplest physical actions such as eating or walking are endowed with meanings that have nothing to do with the dictionary descriptions of these activities. "All situations in the world are figures" (III, 46), claims Witold in *Pornografia*, and Gombrowicz's works well justify this claim.

In *Princess Ivona* eating does not serve to satisfy hunger but to make Ivona choke on a fishbone. The walks taken by Frederick and the narrator in *Pornografia* are not, as they were in the nineteenth-century novels of manners, meant for rest and relaxation; they are surreptitious trips to pick up a dirty and secret letter or to participate in a lustful scene. The double artificiality of *The Marriage* consists in that the whole story not only takes place in a dream, but, within this already unreal framework, is a performance by actors aware of the make-believe situations they enact. Gombrowicz's characters are so accustomed to these double meanings that they cannot take anything at its face value. For Witold and Fuchs in *Cosmos,* cracks in the ceiling are not proofs of shoddy workmanship but secret signs leading to a secret message. For Witold and Frederick in *Pornografia*, the naiveté of the teenagers contains a whole gamut of perverse sexual signs. The meaning of the "figures" in Gombrowicz's universe may be clear to the reader but it is meant to remain at least partially obscure to the characters. Those acts of dissembling performed against some adversary are meant to remain misunderstood by him. Happenings whose source is not explicitly stated in the book are meant to remain obscure to the characters who interpret them. The basic tier of meaning has all but disappeared from Gombrowicz's works. His bewildered characters are surrounded by secrets and they spew out secrets to confuse others and also, ultimately, themselves. The words of every character "only serve to hide something else," as the narrator of *Pornografia* says thus acknowledging his awareness of the necessity of interpretation of the simplest of characters' statements. Nineteenth century narrators were not aware of this necessity. In this respect, Gombrowicz is clearly a post-Freudian writer.

The problem of secrecy brings us close to what Gombrowicz calls "Form." His concept of Form contains the essential ingredients of his vision of humankind. The narrator in *Ferdydurke* spends much time in explaining to us what Form is as do speakers in the *Journal* and *A Kind of Testament.* The idea of Form pervades Gombrowicz's preface to *The Marriage* and shows his kinship to the structuralist concept of literature justifying his jocular statement that he was "the first structuralist" (X, 528). Indeed, his novels can be regarded as written according to a structuralist recipe—some years before structuralism emerged as an important intellectual trend.

Form is the communicative network between people and also the impulse in man compelling him to finish what is unfinished and add to what has already been built. Compelling man to give names, classify and otherwise structure the reality around him, Form arises out of man's will to be. Is it then "equivalent" to what man is? Paradoxically, Gombrowicz says, "No." His books depict the painful struggle of men who feel that Form does not express them fully, and who resent its imposition on their "inner selves." What these inner selves are one never learns; one does gather, however, that there exists in Gombrowicz's heroes some unfortunate "I" which perpetually suffers distortion owing to the omnipresence of Form. This essential part—beyond the reach of words—eludes verbal discovery or verbal communication.

Gombrowicz's intuitions about self and Form are similar to what Jacques Lacan, one of the leading structuralists, has to say about the problems of the distortion of the "I," communication, and language. Lacan in his writings combines psychoanalysis and modern semiotic theory.[10] Starting with Hegel's conception of the master-slave dialectic in the development of the human mind, he traces steps by means of which man attains to consciousness of self. He underlies the existence of a rift between the "the true 'I'" of the unconscious and the "I" articulated by language. The "I" as we know it is expressed by a semiotic system whose roots remain obscure, belonging to the unconscious, while the subject has lost the ability to recognize them. Caught in the web of signifiers, he is unaware of the *prime Signifier* which resides in the unconscious and which, according to Lacan, was arrived at by a series of transformations of the "mirror stage" in the development of the child. When man enters the symbolic order of language, he begins to identify with it. In order to express this identification he carries on the process of naming whose ramifications he continues to pursue. But these chains of signifiers with which man identifies are based on an essential misunderstanding, a fundamental blindness concerning the initial Signifier (which is sexual in nature).

It is enough to replace Gombrowicz's "Form" by "signifiers"

to see that his and Lacan's concept of man have common elements. But, of course, a question of derivation is not involved
since Gombrowicz had not read Lacan when he wrote *Ferdydurke*. Rather, common sources and a proclivity to think similar
thoughts among men of the same generation is responsible.
Gombrowicz's Form arises between men, whom it disfigures
because it does not express what they are in the depth of their
unconscious. It solidifies into a separate reality which threatens
the identity of its creators. Gombrowicz's heroes initially identify
with the signifiers they produce (the Form); later, they notice
that instead of expressing them, these signifiers turn against
them and "fit them with a mug," make them into something
they feel they are not. Owing to "the Formal Imperative," they
continue production of Form, subsequent submission to and
rebellion against it. In doing so they encounter the Form produced by others, the total Form, the culture—which pressures
and disfigures them. In Gombrowicz's world, men generate and
are engulfed by signifiers all at the same time. They are forever
unable to reach toward "the real self," the signified hidden in
the unconscious. This "universal impossibility" is proclaimed by
the narrator of *Ferdydurke* as a condition of human existence.

The emphases in Gombrowicz and Lacan, of course, are different. Where Lacan states, Gombrowicz demonstrates; where
Lacan displays the impersonal curiosity of a scientist, Gombrowicz passionately describes the workings of Form in the lives
of his characters. However, the two men share a perception of
human beings as inevitably lacking in autonomy. Gombrowicz's
characters are unable to exist in isolation from one another. For
Johnnie in *Ferdydurke*, "there is no shelter from the 'mug' except
in another 'mug,' and we can escape from men only by taking
refuge in other men" (I, 276). Henry in *The Marriage* wants to
tear himself away from himself and reach other people. In
Gombrowicz, "the Other" (Lacan's term), though the enemy, is
also desperately needed. Both the desire for maturity and
sublimation and the desire for immaturity and subculture are
oriented toward the same goal—placing oneself in a relation
with others. In Gombrowicz's world, autonomy is a fiction—even
the most autonomous of his characters secretly engage in the
most ridiculous dependencies.

Just as he diverges from Nietzsche and Girard, however, Gombrowicz ultimately parts ways with Lacan to pursue his own vision of the human predicament. In his presentation, man's lack of autonomy and his perpetual incompleteness are not simply deplorable phenomena, but also sources of joy and creativity. Unlike Lacan, he does not merely assert the inevitability of the rift between Form and "the true self" of the unconscious, but taking an unexpected turn says that the suppressed self can after all play a postive role in the dialectic of human development.

IV   The Romantic in Gombrowicz

And here a streak of romantic attitudes in Gombrowicz becomes apparent. The plots of his works—*Operetta* being the most prominent example—contain a suggestion that in man's immature drives and desires there is hidden an ability stubbornly to seek after knowledge, wisdom and joy. Immaturity generates creativity. The refuse rooms of our minds are workshops of our most compelling and powerful ideas. "The sources of my creativity are filled with shame," Gombrowicz says in his *Journal*.

At the center of Gombrowicz's concerns is the paradox of man's ability to put to use what seems mere waste and to transform the ugly and the second-rate into beauty and value. The ability of men to build from out of the meager resources of their imperfect selves never ceases to amaze Gombrowicz. This is why, being an intellectual and elitist writer, he is at the same time also a champion of Mr. and Mrs. Jones's right to celebrate their unsophisticated pleasures. Although recognized as an avant-garde writer, he is an enthusiastic defender of, and believer in, soap operas and "the novels for scullery maids." Sometimes echoing Baudelaire in his fascination for the ambivalence of value and worthlessness, beauty and ugliness, the elevated and the debased, he is opposed to sharp differentiation between the two, characteristic of the ideologically minded. For Gombrowicz, human experience is still a mystery, and no recipe can be given for the artifacts it creates; our best work is born in the impure flame of our petty desires and incompleteness. Gombrowicz pleads the case for the "backyard" of official values and for immaturity because he perceives their significance to man's creativity and ability fully to experience life.

Maturity, for Gombrowicz, tends toward sterility. Our official selves, brought to agreement with "serious" knowledge accumulated by "serious" researchers, tend to be the unproductive parts of our personality. The efforts we make to acquire the semblance of maturity are often destructive of what in man is uniquely creative. And, Gombrowicz contends, these efforts are doomed to fail anyway since "Everything is honeycombed with childishness." To try to live exclusively in the universe of signifiers is an exercise in self-deception. Instead of maturity we achieve expertise at dissembling. Instead of the "I" which we so wish to assert, we end up leading an unauthentic existence, become enslaved to an image of ourselves we wish to maintain in the presence of others.

Immaturity, then, has two ingredients dialectically related to each other. One is the inability to exist or act without in large measure reacting to others. The other is the ability to transcend the psychic wounds unwittingly dealt to oneself in the process of development of consciousness. Gombrowicz feels very strongly about the second and accepts the first defiantly, maintaining that it is inseparable from the second. He rejects the pretensions of those who seek to separate development and achievement from their roots in human imperfection and immaturity. *Operetta*, his last work, expresses these intuitions most clearly. It is an optimistic play. The naked Albertine rises from her coffin to proclaim the victory of youth and nakedness. Her rising gives hope and energy to the entire dramatic society although she is not all innocence and beauty, having been saved by two pickpockets. In *Pornografia* the narrator asks Frederick why they should plot and scheme, and gets the following answer: "For development, dear sir, for development." In the *Journal*, references to development are also common. In 1956, Gombrowicz wrote about "these unavoidable contortions of our development . . . the necessity of reaching one's maximum development," (VI, 238) and in 1966: "Hell is a botched-up enterprise" (VIII, 194). Hell is something that did not come off, in other words, a failure to reach what could have been reached. No development is possible

without enthusiasm, spontaneity, lack of understanding and immaturity according, once again, to Gombrowicz's dialects.

Gombrowicz never fails to avail himself of an opportunity to
demonstrate the desirability of immaturity. His relationship to
his readers is an ultimate instance. Gombrowicz's works are
usually written "against" someone. *Ferdydurke* was an act of
defiance toward critics who accused the author of immaturity.
Trans-Atlantic, Pornografia, and *The Marriage* were directed
against what the author considered the traditional Polish attitudes of patriotism and intellectual docility. The numerous
parodies of living and dead writers were undertaken to defy the
self-assurance with which these writers proffered their vision
of the world. The *Journal* contains many discussions of Gombrowicz's resentments against longtime friends and enemies, and
exposes impulses that can hardly generate a feeling of respect
toward the bearer. Few writers do this—Jean Genet comes to
mind—but in his case the lack of respect is balanced by an
interest which the unusual life of the author evokes in the reader.
We forgive the author his roguishness in thanks for the exotic
psychology we receive. Gombrowicz is unsavory in a much more
commonplace manner. He is a solid, if often impoverished
citizen, and he has never seen the prison yard or experienced the
thrills of a well executed robbery. He lacks Genet's glamor
and he is well aware of it. Yet he exposes his pettiness as if
daring the reader to turn away in disgust. This kind of authorial
courage is rare. "Why does he do this?" wonders Sławomir
Mrożek in his article on Gombrowicz.[12] René Girard might say
here that the author himself is seeking the mediation of his
readers. Like everyone else, he is not free of resentments and
has unsettled accounts which he wants to settle by his making
a statement, writing a book. His action here contains elements of
masochistic reaction since the process of writing is stimulated
by annoyance with others which in turn goads an increase in
the annoyance of others with him. However, to continue with
Girard's terminology, Gombrowicz not only seeks the mediating
presence of his readers but also lays bare his own search for
mediation, thus demonstrating that his dependence on others
is not so pervasive as to blind him to the fact of its existence.
He is not enslaved by it and he produces good work both in

spite of and because of it. In doing so, he transcends the
sterility of masochism and passes onto more fecund ground.

Gombrowicz is, in a sense, the author of only one book, having
basically only one set of concerns. While this is a limitation,
it is a common one. There are few writers who, upon close
inspection, do not turn out to have produced only one set of
characters and only one dramatic situation. Furthermore, to get
the full meaning of Gombrowicz's book one has to read all he
has written, excluding perhaps the early short stories but not
the *Journal*. The dramatic situation he identifies is a complex
one; and if Tolstoy's hackneyed expression may be paraphrased,
all of his works taken together constitute the name of it. Gombrowicz's works form a unity in the sense in which Marcel
Proust's *Remembrance of Things Past* does. Much of what
Proust has to say can already be garnered from the first volume.
The rest is but a continuous re-presentation of the same process
of discovering meanings in the semiotic system of social life.
However, since there are so many meanings to it, the reading of
the subsequent volumes is not a waste of time. A similar thing is
true of Gombrowicz's enactment of the relationship between the
self and the other, and between immaturity as a burden and
immaturity as creativity.

When placing Gombrowicz in some philosophical tradition, it
turns out that while deriving a great deal from a number of
thinkers, he eventually parts ways with them at rather unexpected points. He acknowledges the Nietzschean desire for
autonomy, but at the same time proclaims the impossibility of
autonomy. He endows both the coarse and the refined characters
with the *ressentiment* Nietzsche reserved only for the coarse.
While he converges with Lacan in stressing the pervasiveness
and deceptiveness of Form, he differs from him in that he considers the acceptance of immaturity to be a means of circum-
venting Form. The characters in his books lack self-sufficiency
and are in need of all kinds of help: in that Gombrowicz agrees
with the Catholic tradition in which he was raised. He refuses,
however, to extend supernatural help to his characters, wanting
them to inhabit this earth alone. Gombrowicz converges with the
romantic tradition in hailing youth, enthusiasm and beauty, but

his narrators mock the romantic attitudes which they encounter in their surroundings.

With all his lucidity about man's lack of completeness and his optimism about man's ability to develop, Gombrowicz still does not point toward some perfect way for man to handle the business of living. There are no conversions and no retributions in his works. His most perceptive characters satisfy themselves with the intuition that incessant development is man's most important point of reference. Forever the victims of the split between the "I" and "Form," they nevertheless live on. What saves them from the fate of Sisyphus is that they never get to the top of the mountain and experience the crushing defeat of seeing the stone roll down. They obstinately climb up and while doing so, they believe that their movement is in some way worthwhile, and occasionally even enjoy themselves along the way.

Notes and References

Chapter One

1. "Biographie de Witold Gombrowicz," *Gombrowicz*, eds. Constantin Jeleński and Dominique de Roux (Paris: Editions de l'Herne, 1971), p. 13.
2. *A Kind of Testament*, ed. Dominique de Roux, trans. Alastair Hamilton (Philadelphia: Temple University Press, 1973), p. 28.
3. *Ibid.*, p. 33.
4. Mario Oks, "Trajectoire de Gombrowicz en Argentine," *Gombrowicz*, p. 170.
5. *A Kind of Testament*, p. 37.
6. Tadeusz Kępiński, *Witold Gombrowicz i świat jego młodości* (Cracow: Wydawnictwo Literackie, 1974).
7. *Ibid.*, p. 161.
8. *Ibid.*, p. 290.
9. Dominique de Roux, *Rozmowy z Gombrowiczem* (Paris: Institut Littéraire, 1969), p. 24.
10. Jerzy Jarzębski, "*Opętani*: zapomniana powieść Gombrowicza," *Twórczość*, XXVIII (April 1972), 69–82.
11. On Gombrowicz in Argentina see Zofia Chądzyńska, "Gombrowicz à Buenos Aires," *Gombrowicz*, pp. 186–98; and BOB, "The Unknown Gombrowicz, Playboy and Swinger," *New Horizon: Polish American Review*, No. 3/4 (1977), 14.
12. See also Oks, *op. cit.*, p. 168.
13. Jerzy Cieniewicz, "Gombrowicz au Banco Polaco," *Gombrowicz*, pp. 184–85.
14. In book form it first appeared in French as *Entretiens avec Gombrowicz de Dominique de Roux* (Paris: Pierre Belfond, 1968).
15. *Gombrowicz*, pp. 231–48.
16. Czesław Miłosz, *The History of Polish Literature* (New York: Macmillan, 1969), p. 432.
17. René Girard, *Deceit, Desire and the Novel*, trans. Yvonne Freccero (Baltimore: Johns Hopkins University Press, 1965), p. 263.
18. "Biographie de Witold Gombrowicz," *Gombrowicz*, p. 17.

157

Chapter Two

1. This and the following dates given after the title of the story refer to the year in which the story was written and not to the year of its publication.
2. Andrzej Kijowski, "La stratégie de Gombrowicz," *Gombrowicz*, p. 78.
3. Jerzy Jarzębski, "Między chaosem a formą," *Prozaicy dwudziestolecia międzywojennego*, ed. Boleslaw Faroń (Warsaw: Wiedza Powszechna, 1974), p. 205.
4. Some critics interpret this and the two stories "Virginity" and "Events on H.M.S. Banbury" as primarily sexual. See Jarzębski, "Między chaosem a formą," p. 207.

Chapter Three

1. Constantin Jeleński, "Od bosości do nagości," *Kultura*, No. 337 (1975), 4; and Witold Gombrowicz, "Historia," *ibid.*, 28–55.
2. This has been noted by Michał Głowiński in "Komentarze do Ślubu," *Dialog*, No. 235 (November, 1975), 111–18.
3. The best article on this topic is Louis Iribarne's "Revolution in the Theater of Witkiewicz and Gombrowicz," *The Polish Review*, XVIII, No. 1/2 (1973), 58–76. See also Jan Kott, "Mrożek's Family," *Theatre Notebook: 1947–1967* (Garden City, N. Y.: Doubleday, 1969), pp. 135–42, and Konstanty Puzyna, "Witkacy," in Stanisław Ignacy Witkiewicz, *Dramaty*, I (Warsaw: Państwowy Instytut Wydawniczy, 1972), p. 6.
4. Lucien Goldmann, "A propos d'*Opérette* de Gombrowicz," *Structures mentales et création culturelle* (Paris: Editions Anthropos, 1970), pp. 261–66.
5. On the personality of Ivona see Andrzej Falkiewicz, *Mit Orestesa* (Poznań: Wydawnictwo Poznańskie, 1967), p. 67.
6. Erik Erikson, *Identity, Youth, and Crisis* (New York: Norton, 1968), p. 110.
7. Gerhart Piers and Milton Singer, *Shame and Guilt* (Springfield, Illinois: Charles Thomas, 1953), p. 11.
8. Helen Lynd, *On Shame and the Search for Identity* (London: Routledge and Kegan Paul, 1958), pp. 27–33.
9. *A Kind of Testament*, p. 97.
10. Witold Gombrowicz, *The Marriage*, trans. Louis Iribarne, Introduction by Jan Kott (New York: Grove Press, 1969), pp. 15–16.
11. *A Kind of Testament*, p. 145.
12. Lucien Goldmann, "Le Théâtre de Gombrowicz," *Structures*

mentales et création culturelle (Paris: Editions Anthropos, 1970), pp. 239–60.

Chapter Four

1. The titles of Gombrowicz's novels were conceived with the foreign reader in mind. Two of them: *Ferdydurke* and *Pornografia*, do not require translation into English: *Ferdydurke*, because there is no such word in Polish or in English; *Pornografia*, because the Greek roots of this word are common to English and Polish. *Trans-Atlantic* and *Cosmos* require only two small spelling changes: Polish has *Trans-Atlantyk* and *Kosmos*. The effort to use universal words is also visible in the titles of Gombrowicz's plays *Operetta* and *Historia*.

2. Artur Sandauer, "Witold Gombrowicz: człowiek i pisarz," *Liryka i logika* (Warsaw: Państwowy Instytut Wydawniczy, 1969), p. 151; Constantin Jeleński, "Tajny ładunek korsarskiego okrętu," *Kultura*, 344 (1976), 26.

3. Cesare Segre spoke of the similarity of beginnings in Gombrowicz's novels in "Caos e cosmo in Gombrowicz," *I segni e la critica* (Torino, 1969), pp. 243–50.

4. François Bondy, "Witold Gombrowicz ou les duels d'ombre d'un gentilhomme polonais," *Preuves*, CLXXXIII (May, 1966), 19–30.

5. David Brodsky spoke of the movement from pain at the beginning to laughter at the end in the unpublished paper "Laughter and Pain in Gombrowicz's Fictions" delivered at the Midwest AAASS Conference in October, 1976.

6. Kępiński, *op. cit.*, p. 154 ff.

7. Witold Gombrowicz, *Ferdydurke*, trans. Eric Mosbacher (New York: Grove Press, 1968), pp. 44–46.

8. See Chapter Nine for further discussion of this topic.

9. Artur Sandauer, *Dla każdego coś przykrego* (Cracow: Wydawnictwo Literackie, 1966), pp. 81–169.

10. Bruno Schulz, "Ferdydurke," *Proza* (Cracow: Wydawnictwo Literackie, 1964), pp. 481–91.

11. Gombrowicz, *A Kind of Testament*, p. 69.

12. Czesław Miłosz, *The History of Polish Literature*, p. 434.

13. Artur Sandauer, *Stanowiska wobec . . .* (Cracow: Wydawnictwo Literackie, 1963), p. 38.

14. *A Kind of Testament*, p. 102.

15. Jan Chryzostom Pasek, *Pamiętniki*, ed. R. Pollak (Warsaw: Państwowy Instytut Wydawniczy, 1963), pp. 336–38; Stanisław Urbańczyk, *Zarys dialektologii polskiej*, 5th ed. (Warsaw: Państwowe Wydawnictwo Naukowe, 1976), p. 49.

16. *A Kind of Testament*, pp. 106–107.

17. *Memoirs of the Polish Baroque: The Writings of Jan Chryzostom Pasek*, ed. and trans. Catherine S. Leach (Berkeley–Los Angeles–London: University of California Press, 1976).

18. Stefan Chwin, "*Trans-Atlantyk* wobec *Pana Tadeusza*," *Pamiętnik Literacki*, LXVI (1975), 97–122.

19. *A Kind of Testament*, p. 126.

20. John Fletcher, "Gombrowicz," *New Directions in Literature: Critical Approaches to a Contemporary Phenomenon* (London: Calder and Boyars, 1968), p. 99.

21. *A Kind of Testament*, p. 132 and p. 134.

Chapter Five

1. Witold Gombrowicz, "Przedmowa do 'Trans-Atlantyku'," *Trans-Atlantyk i Ślub* (Warsaw: Czytelnik, 1957), p. 7.

Chapter Six

1. Stanisław Ignacy Witkiewicz, *Insatiability: A Novel in Two Parts*, trans. with an introduction and commentary by Louis Iribarne. (Urbana: University of Illinois Press, 1977).

2. Stanisław Urbańczyk, *op. cit.*, p. 17.

3. Urbańczyk, *ibid.*; and Pasek, *Pamiętniki*, p. 402.

4. Pasek, *ibid.*, p. 421 and p. 336.

5. Giusseppe Ungaretti, "Lettre sur Gombrowicz," *Gombrowicz*, p. 418.

6. A detailed discussion of Gombrowicz's verbal innovations in *Trans-Atlantic* can be found in Krystyna Schmidt, *Der Stil von W. Gombrowicz' "Trans-Atlantyk" und sein Verhältnis zur polnischen literarischen Tradition* (Meisenheim am Glan: Verlag Anton Hain, 1974).

7. The word *upupienie* was first used by Witkiewicz in his novel *Insatiability* (Urbana: University of Illinois Press, 1977), p. 19, but it acquired popularity only after Gombrowicz made it one of the banner words of *Ferdydurke*.

8. On the differences between English and Slavic languages in this respect, see V. V. Nalimov, *Verojatnostnaja model jazyka* (Moscow: Nauka, 1974), chapter two.

Chapter Seven

1. Kenneth Burke, "Four Master Tropes," *The Grammar of Motifs*, (Englewood Cliffs, N. J.: Prentice Hall, 1945), p. 506.

2. In "Anatomia Gombrowicza," *Teksty*, I (1972), 114–32, Jerzy Jarzębski noted Gombrowicz's predilection for speaking about parts of the body, which is also a form of rhetorical reduction.

3. Witold Gombrowicz, *Operetta*, trans. Louis Iribarne (London: Calder and Boyars, 1971), pp. 54–55.

4. Roman Jakobson and Morris Halle, *Fundamentals of Language* (The Hague: Mouton, 1956), pp. 58–82.

Chapter Eight

1. Witold Gombrowicz, *Pornografia*, trans. Alastair Hamilton (New York: Grove Press, 1966), p. 54.

2. Jerzy Jarzębski gives a detailed classification of Gombrowicz's young women in "Gombrowicz i panny," *Odra*, IV (1975), 31–35.

Chapter Nine

1. David Brodsky sees *Pornografia* as a parody of Andrzejewski's *Ashes and Diamonds*. See Brodsky, "Gombrowicz et Nabokov," *Gombrowicz*, pp. 301–24.

2. E. M. Thompson, "Henryk Sienkiewicz and A. K. Tolstoy: a Case of a Creative Borrowing," *Polish Review*, XVII (1972), 52–66.

3. Stanisław Brzozowski, *Kultura i życie*, ed. Mieczysław Sroka (Warsaw: Państwowy Instytut Wydawniczy, 1973). Gombrowicz maintained in his *Journal* that he had never read Brzozowski and that a similarity between his and Brzozowski's views on Polish literature is a coincidence.

4. Constantin Jeleński, "Tajny ładunek korsarskiego okrętu," *Kultura*, 5/344 (1976), 21–32.

5. *Ibid.*, p. 22.

6. F. M. Dostoevsky, *Sobranie sochinenij v desjati tomax* (Moscow: Khudozhestvennaja Literatura, 1958), X, 52.

7. Witold Gombrowicz, *Ferdydurke*, trans. Eric Mosbacher (New York: Grove Press, 1961), p. 218.

Chapter Ten

1. Jan Demboróg, "Inny Gombrowicz," *Tygodnik Powszechny*, No. 2/1459 (1977), 3.

2. Friedrich Nietzsche, *The Birth of Tragedy and the Genealogy of Morals*, trans. Francis Golffing (New York: Doubleday, 1956), p. 180.

3. Friedrich Nietzsche, "Zur Genealogie der Moral," *Werke*, II (Berlin: Gruyter and Co., 1968), p. 284.

4. See note 2, chapter 4.

5. Demboróg, *op. cit.*

6. René Girard, *op. cit.*, p. 4.

7. A letter of Dominique de Roux to Constantin Jeleński, *Kultura*, No. 338 (1975), 155.

8. Witold Gombrowicz, *Pornografia*, trans. Alastair Hamilton (New York: Grove Press, 1966), p. 91.

9. *Ibid.*, pp. 69–70.

10. Jacques Lacan, *Ecrits: A Selection*, trans. Alan Sheridan (New York: Norton and Co., 1977).

11. Sławomir Mrożek, "La Mort," *Gombrowicz*, p. 379.

Selected Bibliography

PRIMARY SOURCES

1. In Polish

Dzieła Zebrane. (*Collected Works.*) in 11 vols. Paris: Institut Littéraire, 1969–1977. This is the most complete collection of Gombrowicz's works to-date. It includes *Ferdydurke* (vol. 1), *Trans-Atlantyk* (vol. 2), *Pornografia* (vol. 3), *Kosmos* (vol. 4), *Teatr* (vol. 5), *Dziennik 1953–1956* (vol. 6), *Dziennik 1957–1961* (vol. 7), *Dziennik 1961–1966* (vol. 8), *Opowiadania* (vol. 9), *Varia* (vol. 10), *Wspomnienia polskie* (vol. 11).

Rozmowy z Gombrowiczem, Ed. Dominique de Roux. Paris: Institut Littéraire, 1969).

The following are first editions:

Pamiętnik z okresu dojrzewania. Warsaw: Rój, 1933.

Iwona, księżniczka Burgunda. Warsaw: *Skamander,* 1935.

Ferdydurke. Warsaw: Rój, 1937.

Trans-Atlantyk. Paris: Institut Littéraire, 1953.

Ślub. Paris: Institut Littéraire, 1953.

Pornografia. Paris: Institut Littéraire, 1960.

Dziennik 1957–1961. Paris: Institut Littéraire, 1962.

Kosmos. Paris: Institut Littéraire, 1965.

Dziennik 1961–1966. Paris: Institut Littéraire, 1966.

2. *English Translations*

Ferdydurke, trans. Eric Mosbacher. London: MacGibbon and Kee, 1961.

Ferdydurke, trans. Eric Mosbacher. New York: Grove Press, 1968.

Pornografia, trans. Alastair Hamilton. London: Calder and Boyars, 1966.

Pornografia, trans. Alastair Hamilton. New York: Grove Press, 1966.

Cosmos, trans. Eric Mosbacher. London: MacGibbon and Kee, 1966.

Cosmos, trans. Eric Mosbacher. New York: Grove Press, 1969.

Ivona, Princess of Burgundia, trans. K. Griffith-Jones. London: Calder and Boyars, 1969.

Ivona, Princess of Burgundia, trans. K. Griffith-Jones. New York: Grove Press, 1970.
The Marriage, trans. Louis Iribarne. New York: Grove Press, 1969.
Operetta, trans. Louis Iribarne. London: Calder and Boyars, 1971.
A Kind of Testament, trans. Alastair Hamilton. Philadelphia: Temple University Press, 1973.
Translations of the *Journal* and *Trans-Atlantic* are in preparation.

SECONDARY SOURCES

1 Books

BONDY, FRANÇOIS and JELENSKI, CONSTANTIN. *Witold Gombrowicz.* München: Deutscher Taschenbuch Verlag, 1978. An analysis of Gombrowicz's plays with pictures of stage productions in Berlin, Zürich, Stuttgart, Bremen and Paris.
JELEŃSKI, CONSTANTIN and DOMINIQUE DE ROUX, eds. *Gombrowicz.* Paris: Editions de l'Herne, 1971. The most complete volume of Gombrowicziana to date. Contains some of Gombrowicz's unpublished texts, an extensive bibliography and several dozen articles and commentaries ranging from family reminiscences to structural criticism.
DE ROUX, DOMINIQUE. *Gombrowicz.* Paris: Christian Bourgeois, 1971. A meditative poem in prose of which Gombrowicz is the central theme.
KĘPIŃSKI, TADEUSZ. *Witold Gombrowicz i świat jego młodości.* Cracow: Wydawnictwo Literackie, 1974. A chatty account of Gombrowicz's childhood and youth by a school friend and a longtime correspondent.
SCHMIDT, KRYSTYNA. *Der Stil von W. Gombrowicz' 'Trans-Atlantyk' und sein Verhältnis zur polnischen literarischen Tradition.* Meisenheim am Glan: Verlag Anton Hain, 1974. A dissertation on the language of *Trans-Atlantic* from the point of view of literary tropes and grammatical categories.
VOLLE, JACQUES. *Gombrowicz: bourreau-martyr.* Paris: Christian Bourgeois, 1972. A psychoanalytical study of Gombrowicz's works.

2. Articles

BARTOSZYŃSKI, KAZIMIERZ. "O nieważności tego, jak było naprawdę," *Nowela, opowiadanie, gawęda,* ed. K. Bartoszyński *et al.,* Warsaw: Państwowe Wydawnictwo Naukowe, 1974, pp. 240–52. The importance of the stage producer for Gombrowicz as opposed to the facts of the narrative.

BŁOŃSKI, JAN. "*Historia* i *Operetka*," *Dialog*, XVI (June, 1971), 86–100. Gombrowicz's *Operetta* is the first philosophical operetta; he created a new genre.

––––––. "Gombrowicz a ethos szlachecki," *Teksty*, IV (1974), 118–36. Gombrowicz's attitudes were shaped by the Sarmatian element of Polish history.

BONDY, FRANÇOIS. "Witold Gombrowicz ou les duels d'ombre d'un gentilhomme polonais," *Preuves*, CLXXXIII (May, 1966), 19–30. An insightful essay on the general features of Gombrowicz's creativity. Discussion of his major works one by one.

BOYERS, ROBERT. "Gombrowicz and *Ferdydurke*: the Tyranny of Form," *Centennial Review*, XIV (1970), 284–312. A coming to terms with the major theme of *Ferdydurke*.

––––––. "Aspects of the Perversion in Gombrowicz's *Pornografia*," *Salmagundi*, XVII (Fall, 1971), 19–46. A subtle argument on sexuality and envy in *Pornografia*. Comparisons between *Pornografia* and Sartre's biographies of Baudelaire and Genet. The best analysis of *Pornografia* yet.

CHWIN, STEFAN. "*Trans-Atlantyk* wobec *Pana Tadeusza*," *Pamiętnik Literacki*, LXVI (1975), 97–122. A detailed comparison of *Trans-Atlantic* and *Pan Tadeusz*.

DEMBORÓG, JAN. "Inny Gombrowicz," *Tygodnik Powszechny*, XXXI, No. 2/1459 (1977), 3. Gombrowicz's *Weltanschauung*.

FALKIEWICZ, ANDRZEJ. *Mit Orestesa*. Poznań: Wydawnictwo Poznańskie, 1967, pp. 57–84. An incisive overview of Gombrowicz's works.

––––––. "Symetryczna męka analogii i analogiczna męka symetrii," *Dialog*, XX (February, 1975), 136–52. On *Ferdydurke*.

FLETCHER, JOHN. "Witold Gombrowicz," *New Directions in Literature: Critical Approaches to a Contemporary Phenomenon*. London: Calder and Boyars, 1968, pp. 95–100. A brief introduction to *Ferdydurke* and *Pornografia*.

GŁOWIŃSKI, MICHAŁ. "Parodia konstruktywna (o *Pornografii* Gombrowicza)," *Gry powieściowe*. Warsaw: Państwowe Wydawnictwo Naukowe, 1973, pp. 279–303. An erudite discussion of Gombrowicz's novels. It is particularly good at pointing out Gombrowicz's predecessors in world literature—e.g., the picaresque tradition in Europe.

––––––. "Komentarze do *Ślubu*," *Dialog*, XX (November, 1975), 111–18. On historicism in *The Marriage*. Głowiński argues that the play is ahistorical.

GOLDMANN, LUCIEN. "La critique n'a rien compris," *France-Observa-*

teur, 6 February 1964. *The Marriage* interpreted as a sociopolitical play dealing with recent Polish history.

——. "The Theatre of Gombrowicz," *Tulane Drama Review*, XIV (1970), 102–12. Also in *Structures mentales et création culturelle*. Paris: Editions Anthropos, 1970, pp. 261–66. A comparison between Gombrowicz's and Genet's theater, and a statement that *Operetta* foretells the 1968 events in Paris.

IRIBARNE, LOUIS. "Revolution in the Theater of Witkacy and Gombrowicz," *The Polish Review*, XVIII, No. 1/2 (1973), 58–76.

JANION, MARIA. "Forma gotycka Gombrowicza," *Gorączka romantyczna*. Warsaw: Państwowy Institut Wydawniczy, 1975, pp. 167–246. Sees Gombrowicz's unfinished potboiler *The Possessed* as a key to his works. Verbose but not void of ideas.

JARZĘBSKI, JERZY. "Anatomia Gombrowicza," *Teksty*, I (1972), 114–32. Parts of human body discussed in Gombrowicz.

——. "*Opętani*—zapomniana powieść Gombrowicza," *Twórczość*, XXVIII (1972), 69–82. An interesting comparison between *The Possessed* and *Pornografia*.

——. "Między chaosem a formą: Witold Gombrowicz," *Prozaicy dwudziestolecia międzywojennego*, ed. B. Faroń. Warsaw: Wiedza Powszechna, 1974, pp. 181–218. Gombrowicz's early works.

——. "Gombrowicz i panny," *Odra*, IV (1975), 31–35. A classification of young women in Gombrowicz's works.

JELEŃSKI, CONSTANTIN. "Witold Gombrowicz," *Tri-Quarterly*, (Spring, 1967), pp. 37–42. A fine introduction to Gombrowicz's works.

——. "Czy 'inny' Gombrowicz?" *Kultura*, 272 (1970), 144–49. A followup to Gombrowicz's correspondence with Jarosław Iwaszkiewicz published in *Twórczość* in 1969. This defense of Gombrowicz gives Jeleński an opportunity to say important things about Gombrowicz's art.

——. "Od bosości do nagości," *Kultura*, 337 (1975), 3–28. An analysis of the play *Historia* published in the same issue of *Kultura*.

——. "Tajny ładunek korsarskiego okrętu," *Kultura*, 344 (1976), 21–32. A bold hypothesis about the relation of *Trans-Atlantic* to *Pan Tadeusz*.

KIJOWSKI, ANDRZEJ. "Kategorie Gombrowicza," *Twórczość*, XXVII (November, 1971), 62–88. One of the finest essays on Gombrowicz by a talented writer and critic. Without ponderous critical terminology, Kijowski manages to get to some of the essentials in Gombrowicz's works. Reprinted in translation in *Gombrowicz*, eds. Jeleński and de Roux, pp. 71–84.

KOTT, JAN. "Ivona comes of Age," *Theatre Notebook 1947–1967.* New York: Doubleday, 1968, pp. 127–30. A lively discussion of *Ivona, Princess of Burgundia* and ferdydurkism.

ŁAPINSKI, ZDZISŁAW. "Ślub w kościele ludzkim," *Twórczość*, XXII (September, 1966), 93–100. On human relationships in Gombrowicz.

MENCWEL, ANDRZEJ. "Antygroteska Gombrowicza," *Z problemów literatury polskiej XX wieku*, Vol. 2, eds. A. Brodzka and Z. Żabicki. Warsaw: Państwowy Instytut Wydawniczy, 1965. Mainly on *Ferdydurke*. Mencwel postulates that *Ferdydurke* contains a grotesque vision of the world, and he brings to bear methods and concepts of recent French criticism.

MIŁOSZ, CZESŁAW. *The History of Polish Literature.* London: Macmillan, 1969, pp. 432–37. A fine discussion of Gombrowicz's place in Polish literature and an analysis of his major works.

——. "Kim jest Gombrowicz?" *Kultura*, 274/275 (1970), 41–56. A profound discussion of Gombrowicz's artistry by a fellow writer.

——. "List do Gombrowicza," *Kultura*, 346/347 (1976), 14–19. Miłosz's argument against Gombrowicz's essay "Przeciw Poetom." This article first appeared in 1951 in *Kultura*.

SANDAUER, ARTUR. *Bez taryfy ulgowej.* Cracow: Wydawnictwo Literackie, 1959, pp. 77–162. A large part of this book is devoted to *Ferdydurke* and its bearing on Polish social and intellectual attitudes.

——. "Witold Gombrowicz—człowiek i pisarz," *Liryka i logika.* Warsaw: Państwowy Instytut Wydawniczy, 1969, pp. 149–82. On the double in Gombrowicz's works and Gombrowicz's antinomies. One of the best essays on Gombrowicz.

SCHULZ, BRUNO. "Ferdydurke," *Proza.* Cracow: Wydawnictwo Literackie, 1964, pp. 481–91. The most insightful of the reviews of *Ferdydurke*; it first appeared in *Skamander* in 1938.

SEGRE, CESARE. "Caos e cosmo in Gombrowicz," *I segni e la critica.* Torino: Einaudi, 1969, pp. 243–50. Points out that the theory of "parts" in *Ferdydurke* corresponds to the economic theory of Gombrowicz's contemporary and compatriot Oskar Lange. A good discussion of Gombrowicz's novels.

THOMPSON, EWA M. "The Writer in Exile: Playing the Devil's Advocate," *Books Abroad*, L (1976), 325–28. On the effect exile had on Gombrowicz.

WYSKIEL, WOJCIECH. "Myśli różne o Gombrowiczu," *Teksty,* VI (1972), 69–84. Gombrowicz's basic themes and the myths about him.

——————. *Witold Gombrowicz: Twórczość literacka.* Warsaw–Cracow: Państwowy Instytut Wydawniczy, 1975. An essay on Gombrowicz's works written for a broad audience.

Index

169